the UP SIDE DE DOWN life

NATHAN WESELAKE

◆ FriesenPress

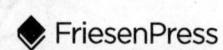

Suite 300 - 990 Fort St
Victoria, BC, V8V 3K2
Canada

www.friesenpress.com

Copyright © 2021 by Nathan Weselake
First Edition — 2021

All rights reserved.

No part of this publication may be reproduced in any form, or by any means, electronic or mechanical, including photocopying, recording, or any information browsing, storage, or retrieval system, without permission in writing from FriesenPress.

ISBN
978-1-03-910187-6 (Hardcover)
978-1-03-910186-9 (Paperback)
978-1-03-910188-3 (eBook)

1. RELIGION, CHRISTIAN LIFE, PERSONAL GROWTH

Distributed to the trade by The Ingram Book Company

the UP SIDE DOWN life

INTRODUCTION

I am here to reassure you.

You need reassurance because you recently decided to follow Jesus, and you aren't sure what you signed up for. You don't know if you have what it takes. Your insecurity is intensified because most everyone around you has been following Jesus since they were children. You started following Jesus last Tuesday.

This late start feels like a disadvantage. Everyone else has a twenty-year-plus head start! No one is rubbing your face in it, but they must see you stumbling along behind them. They must notice how you silently move your mouth, hoping no one catches you bluffing, when the worship leader belts out a song from memory. Even though there are no words on the screen, everyone else is singing along with lyrical precision, and half of them are nailing the harmony.

There are days you think of skipping church, worried they'll go off script like that. It's nearly your worst church nightmare. The scariest scenario is someone asking what the lyrics mean. No one would guess that you have no idea. Your earnest face and outstretched hands indicate you not only understand what you're singing but also deeply desire it. This is not the case. You might as well be singing gibberish. Please, no one blow your cover and ask what the hell "Hosanna in the highest" means. Ahhhh! There you go again—you said "hell!" How long is it going to take before you automatically change to the more appropriate "heck"? All your reflexes are wrong. You still have pagan reflexes.

These people take so much for granted. They not only know every freaking (good job there with "freaking") song lyric by heart, but they know every character in the Bible. You know three: Jesus, Mary, and Jolly Old

Saint Nick. That was a test. If you didn't get it, it means you failed the test. Whether or not you passed this exact test, you know there are significant gaps in your knowledge, vocabulary, and habits due to you being late to the party. This is why you need reassurance. This is why I am here.

Let's begin.

I bet that as you stumble along, putting together the pieces of this new life you're trying to build, it feels like you're doing an old-school jigsaw puzzle. Note that I said, "old school." I said this to ensure you don't see me as a nerd doing puzzles for fun. Nope! I don't even know what kind of puzzles exist today. I'm so cool, I'm totally out of touch with the modern state of puzzles. But I am familiar with "old-school" puzzles because, back in the day, I would do them with my nerdy, nearsighted cousin Aaron and my grandma. Aaron is now barely forty and entirely debt-free thanks to his rigorous discipline. I will do my best to keep my debt-fuelled jealousy at bay, but it may creep out from time to time.

Explaining our strategy for putting together puzzles will help you see that I get how confusing it is to try to piece together what following Jesus means for you. This empathy will also help us bond early in the book as author and reader—unless, of course, you like puzzles. Then I've already burned that bridge. The bridge that spans the river between my coolness and your lameness. It would have happened eventually, so better earlier than later. Maybe you can give Cousin Aaron a text and hang out with him. You'd probably like him better anyway. I swear Grandma did.

I should also say that while I delight in the empathy inherent in the puzzle analogy, I'm aware of its problematic lack of creativity. But this problem will soon go away. Any eye rolls directed at the basic obviousness of the puzzle analogy are premature, as soon I will be adding twists that make it rich, original, complex, and still as empathetic as ever. I don't want to jinx it, but I suspect that never in the history of the written word have originality and empathy been so powerfully combined in a single analogy. So hold off on the eye roll and raise your expectations as high as Grandma's aspirations for Cousin Aaron's career options—which is to say, sky high.

Grandma would set the puzzle box on the edge of the kitchen table so we could see the picture on the box. I can't overstate how helpful this was, as it was a picture of what the assembled puzzle was going to look like. It immediately gave a sense of the general area where a piece might fit. We would begin to connect the border pieces first. They all had a flat edge and were easy to spot and pull out of the pile of pieces. Once we had the border framed out, we started work on the inside of the puzzle. Slowly at first, and then more quickly as the pool of available pieces shrunk, the puzzle would come together.

Now let's add our first twist to this standard analogy. Yes, following Jesus as an adult is like putting a puzzle together. Except this puzzle has no picture on the box, and the pieces can fit together in more than one way. Immediately this makes the task more daunting. I can imagine Cousin Aaron melting down under such circumstances, but you shouldn't. In fact, you be hopeful that there's no picture and that there are options for how to assemble the pieces. This situation might make putting the pieces together more complex, but that's a small price to pay for taking something from mindless task to personal adventure. The increased complexity means following Jesus is about personal discovery instead of being crammed into a mould.

All the pictures are going to look different. How could they not? Diversity must exist because the picture being composed as I put the pieces of my life together with Jesus is going to look different than yours. And, of course, my picture is going to look different than someone's in Australia, Detroit, Croatia, or 1722 Bulgaria—if indeed Bulgaria existed three hundred years ago. These pictures will have something in common, but they'll also be beautifully diverse. There are no stock images in Christianity. We are each becoming like Jesus, yes, but also more like our true selves.

Maybe a recipe is a better analogy than a puzzle. Imagine Jesus inviting you over to cook something together. This sounds good to you. You even ask if you can film it for YouTube. "Cooking with Jesus" has the potential to go viral. What was weird about his invitation was that it included a request to bring all the ingredients you had in your house, but he didn't specify what you were cooking. You found this a bit odd, but it's Jesus, and you're inclined to trust him. Also, he knows what "Hosanna in the highest" means, and you don't. You empty the spice rack, pull everything you can carry from the pantry, and head over to his house. When you get there, he sorts through what you brought. Imagine him whistling to himself and commenting as he rummages through your Trader Joe's re-useable grocery bag.

"Oh, good ... we can use this!"

"Yuck ... no need for that."

"Interesting ... I think that might add a unique twist."

"Get thee behind me, Satan!"

Once he sorts your ingredients, you start cooking together.

The key, as you struggle to keep your head above the surface in the sea of analogies I have you swimming in, is that you're using both his ingredients and yours to make something together. This is another place where the puzzle analogy breaks down. It would be weird for someone to invite you over to do a puzzle and ask you to bring your own pieces to contribute to the picture. The recipe idea is more helpful than the puzzle because it considers your unique ingredients, even if it got kind of weird there at the end when Jesus said that part about Satan.

Let's tie this all together nicely by considering both the puzzle and the recipe together.

Yes, you and Jesus will be working together to assemble and organize the pieces of your life into something beautiful, so the puzzle idea isn't entirely wrong. But the picture coming together piece by piece isn't going to match anything already printed on a box. Rather, it's going to be a one-of-a-kind masterpiece more along the lines of a dish a master chef cooks when he works his creative genius using the available ingredients.

You don't exactly know what it will look like, but you do know that the life you're building with Christ will be uniquely yours because it involves your ingredients and his as you work together to make an edible puzzle. Yes! There it is. An edible puzzle is the perfect analogy. Not to mention a fantastic business opportunity. We should partner in this, you and I, and bring edible puzzles to the hungry marketplace. Fifty-fifty split of revenue. Have your people get in touch with my people. (I have no people; if I did, I wouldn't have self-published.)

Let's summarize what we have covered so far. Following Jesus is kind of like doing a puzzle but also like co-hosting a YouTube cooking show. And by the way, want to be business partners? This has all the hallmarks of a Christian discipleship classic. The saints of old would be proud of this introduction to the Christian faith.

Probably not. However, at this stage my goals are more modest than impressing dead saints, and I believe I have achieved them. My goals all involve you. Are you not considerably more relaxed than you were when you first opened the book? I suspect you are. I should have had you check your pulse so we could compare your beginning of chapter heart rate with now. You are calm. Knowing you are in wise hands. You're subconsciously referring to me as "Uncle Nathan." You are in Uncle Nathan's capable hands—although that phrase might put your heart rate right back up there. Think "kindly old uncle" instead of "creepy uncle."

If you're feeling reassured, I hope it's for four reasons. First, I hope that by now you're getting a sense that this will be fun. By "this" I don't mean reading the book, although how could it not be fun with this high a dad-humour-to-paragraph ratio? What I hope you are sensing will be fun is the journey to becoming like Jesus. He intends it to not be burdensome.

Second, I hope you're feeling better about your relative ignorance about what it means to follow Jesus. It's OK that you don't know what it's going to look like. How could you know that, since there's only one of you? There is no puzzle box. While we could take a fairly accurate stab at what Jesus brings to the equation, we don't know what new creation will emerge as the Jesus-and-you hybrid develops. Following Jesus doesn't turn you into a clone, so we can't tell you exactly what it will look like. Jesus doesn't want clones. He wants hybrids. A new creation that is part him and part you.

Third, I'm also telling you that not knowing exactly what it will look like won't slow down any progress in your new faith. You're not stuck because of a lack of knowledge. This is because your commitment to follow Jesus is primarily a commitment to trust his character and wisdom. It's enough for you to be captivated by him. You don't need to know where you're going, because he knows. You can trust him with that. Your commitment is to follow Jesus step by step, to get to know him better. As you follow him, what you need to do and what might need to change becomes clear. Change, and the power to make a change, comes to you at the right time and in the right way as you walk the path with Jesus.

And change will come. Sometimes the worst parts of you will easily fall away as you respond to the nearness of Jesus in your life. Other times you'll have to muster up some effort and work hard to discard the old ingredients in your life. For every helpful ingredient you bring there might be another that he doesn't need or want as he makes you into a new creation. And, of course, not only do the worst parts of you go, but his presence will enhance the best parts of you. Through this process of enhancing the best and removing the worst, he intends for you to become something you're not yet. This is transformation. This is exciting.

The final reason for you to feel reassurance comes from the fact that Jesus is thrilled you have chosen to follow him, and he isn't worried for a second about you starting your journey later in life. He is similarly thrilled about how he will transform you as you get to know him better. He is also tremendously excited about this book and thinks you should buy several copies of the collector hardcover edition for your friends.

Uncle Nathan is joking. I'm excited for you as well, and it has me giddy. Giddy enough to tell you a classic Christian-insider joke.

Question: "How do we know the early church drove Hondas?"

Answer: "In Acts 3, we read that the disciples were all in one accord."

Honda Accord? Get it? And "one accord" is like "unity." It's a multi-levelled, brilliant gem.

Sigh . . . in some ways, you didn't miss much coming to the party a little late.

CHAPTER 1

Your Mother Tongue

I've played around with various language-instruction apps in the hopes of getting a rudimentary grasp of Spanish, and I've found it frustrating. I don't remember being frustrated when I learned English. This is because I didn't so much learn English as absorbed it. I was immersed in it, and then it flowed out of me without me even thinking. Spanish? I have to think carefully about every syllable, and even then, I end up ordering myself a drink with an umbrella instead of being directed to the bathroom. I've given up and now use crude sign language, pointing to places on my body and raising my eyebrows urgently. It's an effective way to let someone know you need a restroom, although if the eyebrow-raising is misinterpreted as flirtatious and not urgent, it can get complicated. The silver lining is that most jail cells do have a place to go to the bathroom.

My struggle with Spanish won't surprise you. You know that learning things later in life is tougher. You know learning to follow Jesus as a grown-ass adult (there you go again) is going to involve some serious reprogramming of your hardwired circuitry. And even if you do put in the time and start to shift everything that needs to be shifted, isn't it always going to feel a bit imposed? Isn't it always going to feel a bit hesitant, like a role you're playing, or a second language? Won't it be just a matter of time before a moment of crisis or strain has you bursting out in your mother tongue, saying something stupid at best or swearing a blue streak at worst?

You can just see yourself dropping the offering plate onto your toe and yelling painful curses before you can catch yourself.

I can see it too. You're standing there in your summer Sunday best, all red-faced with nickels clattering around your scrawny calves. The young single mom in the row in front of you is turning around and staring at you with a mix of pity and fear. This is truly tragic, because you find her attractive and have been trying to work up the nerve to ask her out. You've hesitated because you're embarrassed about your calves, and now the spilled offering is effectively shining a spotlight on them. Wearing shorts was a poor choice.

But now there is a greater concern than your calves. She has just clamped her hands over her daughter's ears. Not only are you the guy with the disproportionately scrawny legs, but you're also the guy who taught her daughter a new four-letter word in church. The word slipped out of your mouth when the plate slipped out of your hands. You must have said it louder than you thought—considerably louder—since ushers with tasers are making their way toward you. Your fists clench. You can take them. You throw caution to the wind as you roll up your sleeves, even being so bold as to give a wink to the object of your affection. What do you have to lose at this point? Maybe she possesses a rebel streak and could be drawn to the "bad boy" inside of you, if you let him out. Bring it on, ushers. It's about to get real, because the real you is about to come out.

I can see why you might want to avoid this. So let's get started learning how to become a person who doesn't swear in church or brawl with ushers. We'll start with the bar low. Not that this is a specific danger for you, but this weirdly specific example speaks to a broader concern. The concern that you will always be dangerously close to screwing up because you won't be able to hide the real you when life ups the pressure. Sure, when you aren't surprised by a sudden surge of physical pain, or wrestling with strong temptation, it's easy to do what you're supposed to do now that you're a Christian. However, most days include at least one pressure-cooker situation that might cause you to revert to your old, ingrained habits of interaction and response. Your worry is that since Christian behaviour doesn't come naturally to you, and maybe never will, your attempts to follow Jesus will be marked by failure and strain. I can see where you're coming from, but your worry is unfounded.

This concern that Christianity will always feel imposed, or foreign, is one of my favourite misconceptions to correct. The truth is, in a surprisingly short period of time, this new faith of yours will feel second nature. Eventually, it will become impossible for you to scream out cuss words. It won't occur to you, and you won't want to. You'd have to make yourself. All your reflexes flow in Jesus's direction. You'll become the kind of person whose composure the single mom admires. She'll make the first move because you've become that dynamite combo of holiness and sexiness she has been praying for and enjoying vicariously through Sunday afternoon Hallmark movies since her ex ran off with a Democrat.

Jesus is going to change your heart. He is going to go right to your core. Since all your desires, intentions, thoughts, and actions flow out of your heart, it's a smart move on his part. If he can change your heart, then all the exterior stuff you're worried about automatically changes. He doesn't have to correct every little external expression or habit. When the heart is pure, the rest of your life falls in line.

This transformed heart doesn't only lead to changed behaviour but to the personal experience of freedom. Freedom means being able to do whatever you want to do. You don't have that right now, because much of what you want to do would hurt others and yourself. Too often you think to yourself, *If I wasn't a Christian, I'd _____*. You can fill in the blank with whatever forbidden action your heart desires. The point is that there is no freedom when your heart is still desiring things that are immoral, illegal, or otherwise off limits. But as Jesus changes your heart to want the right things, you will experience freedom. You'll be able to do whatever you want. Jesus is bringing you to a place where you can do whatever you want to do because it's good for you and a blessing to others. Christian freedom is the ultimate win-win situation. This is a key thought: Christian freedom doesn't have winners and losers. <u>Make sure you get this paragraph. Re-read it.</u> I kept the nonsense out of it so you could focus.

It probably sounds difficult, but one of the most pleasant surprises as Jesus begins to work on your heart will be how natural the process feels. I've set you up to anticipate it being difficult with my earlier example of trying to learn a new language as an adult. It turns out that example is a poor one because that's not what you're doing as you follow Jesus. Jesus transforming you is less like struggling with a new language than it is like re-discovering a language you already know.

Christianity is your mother tongue.

Imagine a loving immigrant grandmother tucking you in at night as a baby and singing you to sleep in the language of the motherland. She died before you were able to speak to her, so she only exists for you on the edge of your memories. However, every now and then something in your life seems familiar or resonates with unexpected depth because it's connected to your subconscious memories of her. When this happens, you aren't having a new experience . . . you're awakening a previous experience. There are parts of you that remember her.

A similar awakening will be part of your experiences as you grow in your new faith. Yes, there will challenges and confusion along the way. But there will also be a pattern of happy surprises. There will be times when pieces click into place quickly because following Jesus has been bred into your bones. Your affinity for it will affirm that you aren't learning a new language; rather, you're re-discovering your mother tongue. You're learning to understand and speak words that have been spoken over you since before you were in the womb. You're recognizing and remembering as much as discovering. You will find again and again that following Jesus is not a path imposed on you, but something embedded in you. It's what you were designed for.

This idea that following Jesus is what you were made for is a big enough idea to spill a little more ink onto. So let me give you a couple of examples to help drive these truths home. Plus, I like you imagining me with a quill and ink jug, and this gave me a chance to plant that image in your head. Although I'm quite sure it isn't called a jug. I should probably give a quick Google and find the correct term. But I'll leave sorting out that kind of technical detail for the research department of the self-publishing outfit to whom I am paying a small fortune.

Two examples of spilling ink. One nerdy and one warm and fuzzy. The first warm and fuzzy example involves our golden retriever, Penny, technically named "Penelope Bellaferna Junior" by my daughter during a weird

THE UPSIDEDOWN LIFE

naming phase. (She called herself "Peachfuzz Fumblebutts Ariel" for a good three months. The "Peachfuzz" and "Ariel" made sense. Still confused by a five-year-old who wants to be known as "Fumblebutts.") Penny was purchased after considerable research into determining what sort of breed might be best for our family. Research being something I do for every single purchase I make, from winter tires to protein supplements. Research dictated Penny was the dog for us.

I was taken with a few traits bred into Penny: social, gentle, energetic, and with the built-in ability to fetch without chomping down super hard on the item retrieved. I thought this last feature was exceptionally cool, but since I didn't hunt pheasants, it wasn't particularly necessary. What I was into, though, was chucking sticks into the water. Before Penny, I went through so many sticks. They were getting hard to find. I spent more time finding sticks to throw than actually getting to throw them (Exodus 5). The idea of having a dog bred to bring them back to me to re-use was tremendously appealing. I'm joking. Hopefully, you got that and don't see me as some sort of maniacal simpleton chucking sticks in the water for hours on end.

Pretty early on in with Penny, we saw the promised characteristics. She was an energetic extrovert who enjoyed fetching, although it took a bit to get her to release what she brought back. Soon she got the hang of it and was eager to head to the park and play fetch. But what didn't click for her was the swimming part. She was a dry land fetching dynamo, but every stick I chucked into the lake floated away while Penny slammed on the brakes at the end of the dock. She would tap dance her way back off the dock and give me the weirdest apologetic grimace. The same look my dad gives waiters when he's asking them to not put ice in his drink. I wanted a dog that soared off the dock with a splash. I got a tap-dancing, grimacing weirdo. But I didn't give up.

We had many false starts. She ran to the end of the deck and then put the brakes on and broke out into her river dance. I tried tough love. I pitched her into the water. She jumped out as fast as she could and ran away. I tried cupping her face in my hands and saying, "It's not your fault" over and over. People who saw this gave us some extra space. It was nice to have a long stretch of riverbank to ourselves as people kept their kids away, but it didn't help Penny swim.

I don't know what finally did it. Perhaps she was tired of living below her design and call. Perhaps there was the guttural, visceral sound of all her ancestors screaming at her from her DNA to go for it. Whatever it was, there came a day when she jumped. She leaped and landed with a splash. She grabbed the stick and swam back to shore. She was a happy puppy, and I had tears in my eyes. Although not a dog person at all, it remains one of the more powerful events in my life—to see something living far below its design begin to embrace the form and function bred into it by its creator.

If you were to ask me why I'm a pastor, I'd point to the human version of moments like that. To see someone leap into their destiny is to witness a beautiful, mysterious freedom unleashed. Every time I can have a front-row seat for that, I'll take it. It's the heart behind this book.

I feel like the warm and fuzzy example went well. Possibly even had you tearing up ... if you're a certain sort of person. I have to admit, my eyes got a little moist. But it might be the onions I'm slicing. I find slicing onions and writing to be the ultimate multi-tasking feat. Makes me feel really on top of my game as a time maximizer. Now, let's let into the nerdy example.

Every computer, every piece of hardware, has been designed to run on a specific operating system. At the time of my writing, Windows, Android, macOS, and Chrome are the most popular operating systems, and they compete with each other for market dominance. Since they're not friends, there are compatibility issues to overcome if you want a Windows machine to run an Android operating system. Perhaps it can be done with some serious work, but the attempt would be labour-intensive and frustrating—so much so that no one would bother trying except as an experiment to challenge themselves. No one pretends that imposing an operating system on a piece of hardware it wasn't intentionally designed for makes anything better.

However, when you run the appropriate operating system for the device, the whole experience unfolds beautifully. There are specific buttons relevant to the operating system. The integration between the device and the operating system that *animates* it is seamless. Contrast this to an imagined scenario in which a device is running the wrong operating system. Probably the thing doesn't even turn on. This is why it's an "imagined scenario." But say the device does come to life. It would be seriously compromised in its effectiveness. If it were sentient, we can easily imagine that it would have the sense that something is wrong or missing. That it was underachieving in some way. It would be frustrated with itself as much as it frustrated those trying to work with it. Similarly, we can imagine it would feel joy and relief when the right operating system is downloaded and it can be free to be what it was designed to be.

Now, this isn't just the Penny story from a nerdier perspective. It takes it farther. For sure, we can see ourselves as being like the computer, designed by a maker to function a certain way, and when we discover this way, we find ourselves compatible with it and surprisingly suited to it. And yes, there is relief and joy when this way is discovered. But that's the golden retriever story all over again, and there's more to the operating system example than merely revisiting the idea that creation functions best when doing what it was designed to do.

I hinted at what that "more" might be when I intentionally italicized the word "animates" a couple of paragraphs ago to describe how the operating system brings the computer to life. Perhaps this struck you as an odd word to use and, indeed, with computers, it would be. "Animates" is a biological, or spiritual, word more than a mechanical word. It speaks of something coming to life. We use it when we return from a hospital visit and give others an update on who we were visiting, or when a child tells us a story they find exciting. If we were to say, "She was quite animated" about either of those situations, people would know what we're getting at. There is life, energy, and hope in that phrase that makes it appropriate for us to use as we move from talking about computers to talking about you.

The operating system for human beings is the Holy Spirit. Followers of Jesus have the Holy Spirit of God inside of them, animating them and bringing them power. While both the golden retriever and operating system analogies illustrate how you were designed to follow Jesus, the operating system example goes farther and illustrates how following Jesus brings you to life as the Holy Spirit's power moves inside of you. I have confidence you will flourish as a Christian, and my confidence comes because I know what the Holy Spirit can do as it moves inside of you.

Frankly, there are things people with the Holy Spirit can do that those who don't have the Holy Spirit cannot do. As you follow Jesus, you become one of these uniquely powerful, Spirit-animated people, and because of this presence of the Holy Spirt inside of you, everything gets easier. You finally have the right operating system downloaded. The power is inside of you.

This shouldn't just give ME confidence in you—it should give YOU confidence in you. Part of your concern that you won't thrive or be "successful" as a Christian exists because you're not sure if you have enough willpower to do the right thing. But the Holy Spirit isn't willpower. It's the power of God in you. Imagine how much easier it is to change your reflexes when there's a presence inside of you actively harnessing and channelling your energy in a positive direction. The Holy Spirit works in you, mainly in your subconscious, to change you.

What I've just explained here isn't an obscure idea existing on the fringes of Christian belief. As peculiar as these ideas might strike you as, they're core Christian beliefs about what the Holy Spirit does. In fact, we first encounter these ideas in the very first pages of the Bible, and they get refined and developed throughout it. Let's start at the beginning.
In Genesis 2:7 (NLT) we read:

> "Then the Lord God formed the man from the dust of the ground. He breathed the breath of life into the man's nostrils, and the man became a living person."

You immediately see the connection when you understand that the concepts of "spirit" and "breath" are basically the same idea. God breathes his spirit into Adam, and what was only dust is animated and comes to life. Instead of "the man," some translations use "Adam," which reads like a proper name referring to a specific person. But those translations can mislead, since this is clearly intended to be a story about what every human being is like, not just one individual. It's not just that a guy named "Adam" was lifeless until the breath of God entered him. We all are lifeless until the breath of God animates us. This is a story about all of us. Every human being comes to life with this automatic entry-level animation.

I call it an entry-level animation because there's another level of breath and animation. This next level of animation doesn't happen automatically. You have to choose it. It's hinted at in different stories in the Bible, but it isn't until Jesus arrives in the flesh that we get complete clarity on what the hints are pointing to. In perhaps the most clarifying passage, Jesus intentionally picks up on the Adam story but then intensifies and elevates it. Keeping the Adam story in mind, let's look at Jesus's re-enactment of it.

In John 20, Jesus breathes on his followers and says, "Receive the Holy Spirit." It would seem to be an odd thing for him to do. Jesus, with his breath smelling like falafel and hummus, exhaling all over them. Except with the Genesis story in the background helping us interpret his actions, we can see exactly what Jesus is doing. And what he's doing is astoundingly massive. Jesus is re-starting the human race. Not that he's bringing the dead to life in an identical way to Adam's animation, but the notion isn't that far off, because what he is doing isn't any less impressive. He's taking what is already alive, thanks to the breath of God, and giving it an enhanced life, thanks to the infusion of the Holy Spirit. This enhanced life is frequently referred to as *eternal* life and it's characterized by resilience, love, depth, and everlasting duration. Eternal life is the higher level of life that comes with the Holy Spirit. When you commit to following Jesus, this happens to you.

I've been throwing a lot at you. Here's what I want to have stick.

First, Christianity is your mother tongue. You were designed to live this way. It's not a foreign concept imposed on you. Your home of origin is in the heart of God, and every step you take back toward home is going to feel familiar and have a sense of gaining momentum. You're not doing something foreign when you follow Jesus. You're going back to your roots.

Second, the Holy Spirit is given to you when you decide to follow Jesus. This Spirit doesn't just give you physical life, like with Adam. You already have that. Instead, it gives you a life of greater depth and duration, an eternal life like Jesus's. And this power to achieve this life comes from within. The Holy Spirit inside of you empowers you, guides you, and comforts you as it propels you toward your destiny of becoming like Jesus.

It should be no surprise that as you get in touch with your roots (mother tongue) and are filled with new power (Holy Spirit), your life begins to have a natural flow to it. There doesn't have to be any faking on your part because there's nothing artificial happening to you that needs to be propped up. Jesus isn't imposed on you any more than he's imposed on reality. Rather, it was your old life that was out of alignment and it is a lot of work to fight against reality. Now properly aligned, and with the Spirit in you, things can begin to hum. You can start to get somewhere. You feel momentum. Momentum like the Weselake family felt in the mountains of Colorado in 1992.

I was fourteen years old and sitting in the third-row seat as my dad was driving our ancient four-cylinder minivan through the Colorado mountains. The beige beauty was loaded up with five people and enough camping gear to keep us going on a massive three-week, low-budget road trip. At least we hoped it would be three weeks. Our current speed of travel was increasing the length of our itinerary considerably.

We were going very slowly because the mountain passes were turning out to be more than our 1986 Plymouth Voyageur's ninety-six horsepower could manage. Despite revving the engine like it was a chainsaw, we were barely crawling up the mountains. Everything passed us. It was unbearable. Semis. Old people in RVs. The Girl Guide hiking group. Even similar minivans.

It was the similar minivans that puzzled my dad. Why should other beige underpowered minivans be climbing like a mountain goat on the happy side of a case of Red Bull while we lurched along like a mountain goat that just drank a case of vodka? The answer came at a gas station when Dad realized the cheapest fuel in Colorado (and thus what we naturally filled up with) had the octane rating of warm milk. The warm milk wasn't bringing out the best of our minivan engine. When he switched fuel and filled up the old van with the right gas, we shot out of the parking lot and up the freeway, finally able to utilize all of the ninety-six horses at our disposal, and we could even turn the A/C back on. This is what it feels like to be filled with the Holy Spirit.

Yes, I just compared you to an old beige minivan. If it feels underwhelming, that's only because you haven't understood the magnitude of the resurrection joy experienced by our travel-weary family. To be moving with the flow of traffic. To feel the cool breeze of the potent A/C. To have the disturbing oily sheen forming on your sister's neck dry up and disappear. Friend, to compare your future to that glorious moment is to offer you my best image of what it's like when Jesus puts his Spirit in you. Frankly, if that's not good enough for you, then perhaps we should part ways and you can go read something by Max Lucado.

Wait.

Please don't go. I'm not mad. Just a little hurt you might not be as blessed by the minivan analogy as I thought you should be. I tried to make it colourful and engaging. Plus, it represented real vulnerability on my part to offer you a childhood memory. I told you about my sister's oily sheen. Maybe we aren't there yet. Maybe it was a Chapter 5 story and not a Chapter 1 story. Whatever the case, please stay. Max Lucado has so many readers. I only have you, and I am 100 per cent cool with you right now, for the record. The weird issue you had with the minivan analogy is a distant memory for me, and I'm happy to put this unpleasantness behind us.

Let's take a deep breath and move together into the final pages of this chapter and consider what your part in following Jesus might be. Have you considered that maybe you've been sort of a mooch thus far? You simply decide to follow Jesus and then the Holy Spirit comes to you and does all the heavy lifting. Momentum, joy, self control, and purpose all coming your way automatically. Your beige little minivan rocketing effortlessly up hills once too steep to dream of.

Is there not a part of you that has been bracing for when we inevitably talk about what Jesus is going to demand from you in return? That time has come. Jesus does have something he wants from you. Brace yourself. He wants consent.

Wait. That doesn't seem so bad. A little weird maybe, given the ways consent is often used, but all the more memorable because of it. And if given the choice between "forgettable but comfortable" and "memorable but awkward," old Uncle Nathan is going to go with the latter ten times out of ten.

Your part is to give consent. You need to give Jesus permission. Your transformation depends on him. Permission depends on you. The link between transformation and permission is clearly seen when you consider the different types of Christians you know.

I presume you know inspiring Christians. Those who have something profoundly beautiful going on. There is an effortless grace to their lives. They possess personal power and are living according to their design. But you also know confusing Christians who say they follow Jesus, but you would never guess. They are angry and inconsistent. They show little evidence of momentum or power. They don't inspire with visions of what is possible. To use a full and multi-dimensional word like "eternal" to describe their life is a stretch. "Fragile" is a more fitting word. Something is missing.

What's missing is the flourishing that comes as a by-product of consent. The difference between the two types is that one is faithfully partnering with Jesus, and the other isn't. The "confusing" regularly say "no" to following the example and advice of Jesus, and the "inspiring" always say "yes." You get as much of Jesus's transformative power as you want, and when you've decided you've had enough, your life stops inspiring and begins confusing.

Until you think it through, it might feel intimidating to realize how important consent is. But again, that means you're thinking of consent in the context of pressure and persuasion. You're imaging having to continuously give permission to Jesus to do things in your life you really would rather not have done. This scenario makes Jesus like a pushy immature boyfriend, and that's not an accurate scenario. Jesus is not a pushy, immature boyfriend whose intentions you can't entirely trust. No. You can trust Jesus. His love for you is unfathomable, and his intentions for you are beautiful. This makes consent easy. You grant consent to Jesus happily and easily because you want to. Consent is motivated by desire, not pressure. You desire to know Jesus and become like Jesus. He has captured your heart. This is the proper emotional response to the cross.

The fact that desire is key is reassuring. You thought you needed a specific skill set, vocabulary, or moral code to follow Jesus well. Turns out all you need is desire. The desire to become like Jesus and the permission you give him, which flows out of that desire.

It's critical for people who have been Christians for a while to be reminded of this. Too often, when someone else has an experience of

Jesus's presence or power that they haven't had themselves, they wonder why Jesus is playing favourites. They wonder what they're doing wrong. Often they can't find anything glaring, and this makes them bitter, as they imagine Jesus as unfair. Rather than lament what they perceive as unfairness, they would do better to consider what areas of their lives they have denied Jesus access to, even asking Jesus where they have blocked his work in their life. Jesus has no favourites, only those who have opened the door wide to him, and those who have slammed it shut. You get as much of Jesus as you want. Desire is key.

Should one of these frustrated Christians courageously ask Jesus what the problem is, they'll find that Jesus answers quickly. Jesus knows where we are saying "no." He wants to transform us, sees where we are hurting ourselves, and is kind enough to point his finger at the offending areas if we ask. But we need to ask. Which, of course, we won't hesitate to; otherwise, we risk the ludicrous situation in which Jesus has said to us "Follow me!" and we nod enthusiastically but don't move toward him an inch. You can't follow Jesus and stay where you are. You have to go with him in the direction he is going. You have to be about the same things he is about. You bend your will to his. You give him authority over you. This we have called consent.

Often our resistance is subtle. One subtlety is especially common for new Christians. Let's bring it into the light so you can be ready. What you need to be ready for is the temptation to shift Jesus into the role of genie, to make him into someone who has arrived to grant your wishes. This shift is predictable because it's easy to assume that the power and momentum he offers are tools given to us to build our lives as we choose. He gives us the power and momentum we need to make our dreams come true, right? This is not the case, and when we think it is, we end up miserable because we think we've been lied to.

The new Christian's six-month to three-year predictable lament is "I thought God was going to _____, but he never did." Fill in the blank with an unmet specific expectation she thought should have happened in her life but didn't. This disappointment causes the new Christian to recoil a bit from Jesus and makes further consent difficult. Eventually, there is some distance and drift. Before she gets very far, she pulls the plug, frustrated that God didn't make her dreams come true. Recognize this when it happens to you. It is a rite of passage. It might be the first test of your new faith. Part of your new faith is to hold on to the truth that God's dreams are bigger than yours and better for you than yours are. Indeed, part of giving Jesus consent, and really what you agreed to when you said you would follow Jesus, is agreeing to swap out your dreams for his.

Jesus's invitation of "Follow me" could be rephrased as the question, "Will you swap out chasing your dreams for chasing mine?"

Now listen, this giving up your dreams, this direct pursuit of your happiness, might sound like an invitation to misery, but it isn't. No, you directly pursuing your happiness is what was making you most miserable in your life. The phrase from Alcoholics Anonymous offered when someone starts rationalizing his behaviour or second-guessing the program is helpful here. The addict is reminded by the group that "Your best thinking got you here." There's a sobering wake-up call about our own limitations in this phrase—like maybe you don't really know what will make you happy. Or even more thoughtfully, perhaps Jesus is saving you from the hell that will come your way as you, in your ignorance, chase what you think will make you happy.

Jesus understands what makes human beings tick, what makes them fulfilled, and yes, what makes them happy. You're going to have to trust that he knows what he's doing. This trust will be tested, especially in the times when you aren't exactly seeing personal ambitions moving from dream to reality. But if you can manage to trust him, you'll find that personal happiness is the by-product of following Jesus. When you stop trying to do what you think will make you happy and begin doing what makes Jesus happy, personal happiness finds you. Happiness sneaks up on you as you move with Jesus to make God's dreams come true. Remember all this when Jesus doesn't seem to be helping you make your dreams come true. That isn't what following him is about. And your dreams aren't what make you happy, anyway. Making God's dreams come true is.

Your happiness lies in making God's dreams for planet Earth become a reality.

This is what you were created for (mother tongue, operating system).

This is why you have the Holy Spirit (power and animation).

Your destiny is to make the dreams of God come true. Since fulfilling your destiny generally feels pretty darn good, you can expect to find happiness as a by-product. Remember Penny sailing off the dock and into the water for the first time? Imagine her emotional state as she surfaces after the jump as design, longing, and function click into an alignment not enjoyed before. This is what is waiting for you.

And while the lack of clarity about what God is dreaming about might cause a tad bit of wariness at this stage, let me reassure you. You won't be wary for long. The specifics of what God is dreaming about are as appealing as they are spectacular.

CHAPTER 2

The Dreams of God

What Is God Dreaming About?
The Bedtime Story Edition

Let Uncle Nathan tuck you in. I'll just establish myself on the foot of your bed. Adjust my cardigan. Put my reading glasses on my nose. Light up a joint. And off we go. Kidding.

There once was a world where everything worked pretty well. Cars rolled along on their wheels.

Houses had stairs at the front, and you could easily go in the door.

People walked on their feet.

No one's heart hurt.

No one's head was red.

Everyone could swallow their food easily.

Then an evil wizard came along and pushed everything over a cliff.

It was a long, long, long fall, and the crash at the bottom did two things.

First, it knocked everyone unconscious. Everyone fell asleep.

Second, it flipped everything over.

The houses sat on their roofs.

The cars sat on their roofs.

The trees grew backward.

When people woke up, they stumbled to their feet and looked around. They saw everything flipped over, but they didn't know it had flipped over, so they just assumed that was how the world was supposed to be.

Everything was wrong, but they didn't know.

So they started walking on their hands. I don't know if you've ever walked on your hands before, but it's hard, and it was hard on them.

Their tummies started to get sore.

Their heads turned red.

It was really hard to swallow their food.

It felt weird, but since it was the only world they could remember, they thought it was just normal.

Normal? For houses to be on their roofs?

Normal? For cars to be on their roofs?

To have to walk on your hands?

To almost choke on your food every time?

Every now and then, someone would say, "My head feels like it's going to burst!" or "My tummy really hurts!" But they didn't know why, and they didn't know what to do.

Then one day someone came along who was different. They thought he was really weird. He was walking on his feet. He was turning things over. He was replanting the trees the right way. He was putting cars back on their wheels. His head wasn't red. His tummy didn't hurt.

They all said to him, "What are you doing, you crazy guy?"

"Trees aren't supposed look like that. Cars aren't supposed to be on their wheels. Why isn't your head all red?"

"You aren't supposed to walk on your feet."

They were so used to everything being wrong that they thought wrong was right! They told him he was turning things UPSIDEDOWN, but he was just putting them back the way they were supposed to be.

Soon there were lots of people watching him. He had a crowd following him everywhere. It looked kind of funny. One guy standing on his feet and a whole crowd around him standing on their hands, with their red faces trying to see what he was doing.

He said to them all, "Who wants to get turned UPSIDEDOWN?"

Some of the people wanted to, so they came to him and he put his hands on them and flipped them over. They thought it was awesome. They could drive their cars! They could climb trees! Their heads weren't red anymore. They could swallow their food and not choke.

You'd think everyone would want to be turned UPSIDEDOWN by this man, but not everyone did. Some people had lots of money and were scared it would fall out of the buckets they carried it around in if they got turned UPSIDEDOWN (which is really the right way).

Some people who had lots of power were scared they might fall off their thrones if they got turned UPSIDEDOWN (which is really the right way).

Some people who had lots of attention were scared people would have more interesting things to pay attention to when they could see all the new things you can see when you're standing on your feet.

The people who didn't want to turn UPSIDEDOWN (which, of course, is right-side up) got very worried and angry. So they captured and tried to stop the man who was turning things back the way they should be. They put him in prison and threw away the key.

It was sad for all the people whom he had turned UPSIDEDOWN, but they weren't sad for long. After just three days, the man escaped from prison and went and visited his friends. He gave them a very special and important message.

He said, "I'm going away for a while. You can't come with me yet because I need you to finish what I started. I'm going to leave you in this world where I've turned some things UPSIDEDOWN and some things are still broken. But just like I went around turning things over, I need you to put your hands on everything you can and turn it UPSIDEDOWN (which is really the right way). You do as much as you can. When I come back, I'll do the rest, and then we'll have a huge party."

What Is God Dreaming About? The Grown-up Version

I told that story to a group of grades 1–4 students, and while I expected the kids to like it, I was surprised that the smattering of parents and teachers present liked it as much as they did. They gave me a standing ovation. I had to come out for an encore and sang "Sussudio" by Phil Collins, which they loved much less. They loved the story because although most were followers of Jesus, they had forgotten God has a dream for planet Earth, and they had forgotten how central their role in fulfilling that dream is. It isn't just new believers who can have their vision of what God wants to do shrink to being not much bigger than personal health and happiness. But narrowing God's dream to the "American Dream" ceases to inspire us. What inspires us is being in sync with the heart of God. When we begin to imagine that God is as excited about Costco coupons as we are, our lives sink into redundancy and boredom. To be reminded that God's dream is as big as reality, that he dreams about turning the world UPSIDEDOWN, and that he created and commissioned you to make his dreams come true is life-giving, because it rescues you from a banal existence.

God's dream elevates you out of the unthinking drudgery of the mundane. God's dream refocuses your vision and imagination. Think of all the ways tummies hurt and faces are red: hunger, abuse, inequality, shame, and anger. God's dream is to fix this all, and he created you to help him. Jesus breathed on you to uniquely empower you to help him. This would be thrilling all on its own, but then add in that it leads to your happiness and you have to admit that it is all arranged in an exceptionally gracious way. Especially when you consider that he could have theoretically set it up so that making his dreams come true makes you miserable, but he didn't. Your happiness and his dreams are compatible and connected.

That's the bedtime story and the grown-up version. Uncle Nathan has long since stood up from his perch at the foot of your bed, tussled your tired head, and kissed you on the forehead. However, you are still lying there like a wide-eyed owl mulling things over amidst the residue of the sweet stench of my three-dollar cigars and old man smell. You have lots on your mind.

You are skeptical. Perhaps because anyone who pitches "win-win" in your life has been flat out lying to you. Or maybe your skepticism exists because you realize it isn't a far leap from "living for the dreams of God" to doing something "in the name of God," and there has been a tremendous amount of suffering linked to that last phrase. You don't want to become a religious fanatic.

Or maybe you're worried. You feel like if God sets you loose to make his dreams come true, you won't know what to do, or you'll do it wrong, and the dream could become a nightmare.

Maybe what's making you toss and turn is curiosity. You appreciate the depth of poetic images like "tummies" and "red faces" but wonder what exact form that takes in your life.

Ah, you poor mess of skepticism, worry, and curiosity! No wonder you can't sleep. Thankfully, Uncle Nathan has just come back into the room with a nice warm cup of apple cider vinegar, water, and honey, mixed in a precise sleep-giving ratio. But since this elixir won't kick in for about fifteen minutes, he also brought his Bible so he can show you with more precision what exactly God is dreaming about and how you fit in.

Let me just sit here on the foot of the bed again and tell you about God's dream. I'm doing this against my better judgment, because I hate it when people tell me their dreams. People telling me their dreams puts me to sleep. Especially my foster son, for whom the sake of preserving his anonymity I will call "Truffles." Most every morning, Truffles tells me his dream from the previous night. He starts over breakfast prep and doesn't stop until I boot him out of the car at school an hour and a half later. His re-telling is detailed enough to both drive you insane and make you marvel at the minutiae he remembers. He remembers every single detail. I've risked speeding tickets trying to get him to school earlier so I didn't have to hear which Marvel character was unmasked and found to be his friend, Deshawn, and how his grandma was there as well, cooking bannock, and Ms. Dalrymple was riding a unicorn, and Thanos was playing "Stairway to Heaven" on the guitar while Truffles himself fought off a wolf pack so he could rescue the Golden Saxophone from the Smurfs. Yes, I have checked under his bed for LSD.

God's dream for planet Earth won't be as rambling and confusing as old Truffles when he starts going, and you'll like both the plot line and the details. I know you'll be nicely engaged as you hear it, because it involves you. Even my weary ears pick up a bit when Truffles says, with a mouthful of toast, "You were in my dream last night." We're drawn to plots that involve us, even if we aren't the primary actor. (In Truffles' dreams, I'm usually a bit character down on his luck and selling lemonade or dancing to make ends meet. Occasionally, I'm in the hospital. I discourage you from interpreting those images.) You'll not only like God's dream because you're in it, but also because it's going to come true. It isn't random fiction inspired by last night's bedtime poutine. It's a true story. As you begin to see how the hurts of the world, including your pain, are truly going to be healed, you'll be automatically engaged and powerfully moved.

Let's begin, then, to see exactly what this UPSIDEDOWN dream is.

Anastatoo

You've probably noticed I've been using ALL CAPS to write the word UPSIDEDOWN. Given the "every single word counts" intentionality I've demonstrated thus far, you know I've capitalized UPSIDEDOWN on purpose but aren't sure why. It's probably driving you crazy. Probably you're salivating. Well, salivate no more! Actually, sometimes you can salivate. Salivating is a truly a grey area in Christian discipleship and we have to guard against black and white legalism.

There are four reason I type (Type? Yes, type. That quill and jug bit from earlier was nonsense, and you knew it.) UPSIDEDOWN in ALL CAPS. First, to sear it into your brain. Second, it lends itself better to UPSIDEDOWN™. Trademarking my brand is critical for creative control over movie script and merchandising, especially in the dog-eat-dog world of high stakes self-publishing. Third, it lends itself to incorporation. As an employee of "UPSIDEDOWN Incorporated," I'll be on stronger legal ground and poised to withstand the anticipated lawsuits from Cousin Aaron, Max Lucado, Southern Baptist Convention, Grandma, and Truffles. Fourth, like the lemons I squeeze in Truffles' dreams, I'm going to be squeezing every bit of juice out of the word UPSIDEDOWN for the rest of this book, and what I'm going to do with it means I have to write it like that.

Amidst your roaring laughter, you probably realized that was unsatisfying as an explanation since it raises more questions than answers. But that is all I can say right now if I'm going to stay true to the overarching artistic vision of this book. What I can say is that if you're patient, you'll eventually be satisfied with where this goes. Now please don't read that as a "money back" guarantee. Heavens, no. I encourage you to see my guarantee of satisfaction as more of an evasive and vague promise to buy me time than a literal guarantee. Better yet, see the promise as not from me, but from UPSIDEDOWN Inc.

Since we'll be getting so much juicy mileage out of UPSIDEDOWN, it might surprise you that the word only appears three times in the Bible. It's an odd place to camp if you were looking to settle on a concept to explain the dreams of God. You might suspect a better place for me to pitch my tent would be "Kingdom of God" or "grace" or "church" or "worship" or something more obvious. But you'd be wrong. Kidding. I appreciate and value your opinion. But then again, you are a new Christian, so I can probably choose any old word and fool you into believing that it's of central significance. Not that I would do that, or that it would even occur to me.

Making my choice of UPSIDEDOWN even more suspect is that while UPSIDEDOWN does appear three times in the Bible, you might not see it three times. If you read a Greek manuscript of the New Testament, you'll see the word *"anastatoo"* three times, but only occasionally is it translated as "UPSIDEDOWN." It depends on the English translation of the Bible you're using. So yes, a significant chunk of this book is centred on a relatively obscure, barely used word that can be translated a few different ways into English. However, its relative obscurity and variety of translation options don't keep it from being immensely helpful. Soon you will share my bouncing enthusiasm about this rare word. Besides, you're already nearly thirty pages in and more or less committed to reading the rest.

Two of the three appearances of anastatoo occur in the book of Acts and one in Galatians. We'll spend most of our time on a specific spot in Acts, but it's helpful to look at the other two places to get a sense of the ways this word can be used before we zoom in on our use of it.

In the section of Galatians featuring anastatoo, the Apostle Paul is using strong language to correct a church community whose priorities are out of whack. He's chewing out the church for forcing new people to make unnecessary lifestyle changes. "Lifestyle" is the right word for most of the changes, like if your church made you shop local, stop smoking joints when you tuck your nephews in, or get a haircut before you could participate in church things. Some of what the Galatian church is insisting on are proper lifestyle changes, and Paul is OK with those. But lifestyle doesn't quite do justice to the most intense requirement some in the Galatian church are insisting on, and this is the one Paul has a big problem with. They are insisting that grown men get circumcised.

This isn't as randomly sadistic as it appears. The first Christians saw following Jesus as an extension of Jewish faith, and to be a faithful Jewish man meant you had to be circumcised. For Jews, the role of circumcision was clear—males weren't part of the people of God if they were uncircumcised. If we give the hardline Jews Paul is arguing with the benefit of the doubt, we admit they could be motivated by a desire to be faithful rather than trying to keep their club exclusive. But Paul doesn't care about their motivation. They're wrong and causing problems.

We understand these early stories in the Bible better when we remember that the first Christians didn't see themselves as part of an entirely new religion. They didn't think of themselves as Christians, and they weren't even called "Christians" until about about seven years after Jesus's resurrection. Early on, they were exclusively Jews who followed the Rabbi Jesus. Many New Testament stories are about figuring out what essential parts of the Jewish religion remain necessary practices for those who now follow a very different rabbi. Jesus was a rabbi who claimed to be the Son of God, whom God raised from the dead, and who sent the Holy Spirit to empower them. It takes a while to work out the implications! Some traditions they end up hanging on to, and some they let go of. The mandatory circumcision policy needs to be let go of. Paul is adamant.

In Galatia, grown men are getting circumcised. The way Paul is writing makes it clear that people in Galatia want to belong to this new Jesus community so badly that they're doing whatever it takes to get in. Some are, anyway. It's not hard to imagine that not everyone is willing to do this. Also not hard to imagine that the public relations side of this is not helpful. Buzz around town is that if you want to join this weird new cult, you have to go under the knife. No matter what angle you view the issue from, it's clear that circumcision is a barrier for those wishing to follow Jesus. When people put unnecessary barriers between others and Jesus, Paul gets livid, as should we. When Paul gets ticked, he is devastatingly clever with his pen. Check out his response to the mandatory circumcision group in Galatians 5:12. I'll offer my own paraphrase of the verse because it captures this cleverness better than most translations:

"I wish those people who are troubling you by insisting on *cutting around* (circumcision) would themselves be *cut off* (castration)."

The play on words and visuals created are intentional and show Paul to be as clever as he is forceful, as humorous as he is poignant. Remind you of anyone? No? Oh, um, me neither.

Our attention is naturally drawn to the graphic imagery of the verse, but that is not the place to settle. What we are supposed to be looking for is anastatoo. Did you see it? Here is a clue: the first glance we take at anastatoo is troubling. Literally. Part of what it means to turn the world UPSIDEDOWN is to make trouble of some kind. Now, "troubling" isn't the fullest meaning of anastatoo, and it isn't right to imagine Christians as renegade troublemakers, or that God's dreams for planet Earth are troublesome. But we get a hint here of the intensity, disruption, and change those who follow Jesus will bring.

"Trouble" is a relative term. Trouble for the fat-cat factory owner happens when the union advocates for fairer pay, but this isn't trouble for the workers. No, it's hopeful. Trouble for the criminal is justice for the citizen. Trouble for the human trafficker is hope for the slave. Trouble for the aggressor is safety for the victim. Trouble is a relative term depending on which side of the word you're on. Peacemakers can simultaneously be troublemakers. We see this peace–trouble tension in the other two places anastatoo is found.

In Acts 21:38, Paul instigates a mob riot and is arrested for his protection. The Roman army swoops in, taking Paul into protective custody. Before they entirely remove him from the scene, he asks the commander's permission to address the mob. Paul, bruised and bloodied and being hauled off to a secure facility, has the composure to tap the commander on the shoulder:

"Um . . . pardon me, sir. Could I say a few words?"

There's a captivating authority Paul displays in moments like these. He does this more than once. There is absolute mayhem all around him. In this case, the mob is screaming, "Kill him! Kill him!" Yet he manages to catch the eye of the most powerful person. He not only gets his attention but frequently gets him to do what he says. That's what happens on this occasion. The commander grants his request to speak to the people who've been trying to kill him.

But before he hands Paul the microphone, the commander expresses surprise that Paul speaks Greek. He thought Paul was an Egyptian leading a band of 4,000 in a rebellion against Rome. I'm not making it up: "Aren't you the Egyptian who led a rebellion some time ago and took 4,000 members of the Assassins out into the desert?" (Acts 21:38 NLT).

Paul probably didn't find this as funny as I do. The commander may have been a fine leader of men, but he doesn't seem to be much of a detective. He might be good at crossword puzzles, though, because he uses just the right word. In Acts 21:38, the word translated "rebellion" is our favourite Greek word, anastatoo.

These two situations are clearly different from each other. But as different as they are, we end up looking at anastatoo from pretty similar angles in both, and we see some pattens emerging. Again, we don't want to get too excited, or worried, that the primary task of a Christian is to cause trouble. But we also don't want to miss that a travelling preacher could be mistaken for someone attempting to lead a large rebellion. While the commander is wrong about the type of rebel Paul is, he's not entirely wrong about him being a revolutionary. And while it's hard to imagine your pastor getting arrested in the church parking lot due to being accused of leading a revolution, these two looks at anastatoo might begin to make you wonder if perhaps it shouldn't be as hard to imagine as it is.

The final place we see anastatoo is the most illuminating. It's most helpful for us because while the situation is somewhat like the riot scene described above, there's more of a backstory available. Anastatoo appears in Acts 17:6, but we'll pick up the story in Acts 15 as Paul and his sidekick, Silas, arrive in the city of Philippi determined, as always, to spread the message of Jesus. Their usual strategy in a new community is to find the local Jewish synagogue and show how the life and teachings of Jesus are the extension of beliefs the Jews already hold. You remember this from the circumcision controversy (although you tried your best to forget).

Since the Jews are already anticipating a Messiah, Paul simply has to show them that Jesus is who they are waiting for. In a way, his arguments are a bit like my "mother tongue" idea earlier. He helps them see that while Jesus seems like a new idea, and following Jesus is going to be different, Jesus is an embodiment of the best parts of what they already believe. In Philippi, they can't use their usual strategy of starting at a synagogue, because Philippi doesn't have a synagogue. There aren't enough people who follow the Jewish faith to have one, but there does appear to be a cluster who meet by the river. Jewish religious practise requires frequent ceremonial washing, and a river is an ideal place when you don't have a synagogue with the appropriate tanks and basins. Tanks as in tanks of water, not as in twentieth-century artillery. Just keeping you from mistaking Paul as a tank commander. A surprisingly honest mistake, as the second use of anastatoo showed us.

Paul and Silas head to the river and start chatting with the little congregation there. Out of this first conversation, a woman named Lydia is baptized and follows Jesus. She offers to give our two heroes a place to stay. A conversion and free room and board in one day is pretty much every pastor's dream day. The two men, giddy at their good fortune, stay at Lydia's house and use it as a home base for their missionary work in Philippi.

Their daily commute involves passing a slave girl whose owners have her running a fortune-telling booth. It isn't a scam. She is demon-possessed and has insight into the unseen realm. When Paul and Silas pass her, she screams, "These men are slaves like me! But of the highest God! They will proclaim to you the way of liberation" (Acts 16:17b The Voice). Paul and Silas don't care for this part of their commute. Kind of like that merge you dread with the short on-ramp coming off the cloverleaf onto the busy freeway. You don't have a demon-possessed slave girl howling at you, but you are cursed by the lack of horsepower in your 2011 Corolla. Then, as now, there are parts of our commute we can do without.

It might surprise you that they didn't care for her howling. You might think they'd be OK with the free advertising. Isn't all publicity good publicity? Paul and Silas don't think so, and it's hard to blame them. Making a demon-possessed slave girl your brand spokesperson is the kind of idea that has you switch advertising agencies. Can you imagine the pitch?

"So . . . what we're thinking is . . . wait for it . . . wait for it . . . we get old Mary here, who is certifiably bonkers, and get her standing at the street corner, where she screams her head off about your product! Yes . . . I know. Don't you love it?"

We don't know how many days they hustle past her, but eventually Paul gets frustrated and performs an exorcism. He casts the demon out of her in Jesus's name. We don't know why he didn't do it sooner. Maybe her masters treated her well enough that Paul didn't feel a pressing urgency. Or maybe, like us, it sometimes takes Paul a while to do the right thing. Most likely, Paul wanted to fly under the radar of the city officials for a while and knows if he frees her from demonic oppression, he's going to get some unwanted attention.

Paul is right. As soon as he casts the demon out of her, she's no longer able to tell the future, effectively drying up her owners' source of revenue. They're furious and publicly accuse Paul and Silas of spreading an anti-government message. The charges are a bit of stretch, but the city officials buy it, and Paul and Silas are arrested, beaten, and thrown into jail—all without a trial.

While in jail, Paul and Silas begin to sing and pray, demonstrating the kind of personal power possible because of the Holy Spirit. They've been beaten with clubs, left unfed, and put in stocks, freezing them into a torturous position. That they are singing and praising despite their condition is a miracle. But it's not the only miracle that night. At midnight, an earthquake knocks over the walls and breaks the chains, setting the stage for an easy escape for all the prisoners. The jailer panics, because an unwritten but clearly understood clause in his contract states that he's dead meat if any prisoners escape. These were the days before the prison guard union rep managed to secure a solid healthcare package, three weeks of vacation, and early retirement for union members.

To escape the certain shame, likely torture, and possible death resulting from allowing the escape, the jailer decides to take his own life. He is basically in the act when Paul stops him. Paul has kept all the prisoners from running away. We don't know how Paul did this. Perhaps he promised to get them cigarettes from the outside or increase the frequency of conjugal visits. Regardless of what Paul had to do to pull it off, the unexpected kindness speaks volumes to the formerly sadistic warden, and he transforms into a kind man. Soon jazz music is playing over the prison PA, and each prisoner is enjoying a nice cold long-necked beer. Actually, what happens is better than that. Paul baptizes the jailer and his family, and then, in a display of gratitude and tenderness, the jailer personally dresses their wounds.

Come daylight, the officials of the town show up and appear ready to take things with Paul to the next level. Paul then plays an ace up his sleeve—he tells them he is a Roman citizen. This is a big deal. Roman citizens sit at the very top of society's food chain, and there's no way a Roman citizen like Paul should have been beaten and incarcerated without a fair trial. The officials are in big trouble.

If I'm Silas, I'm wishing Paul had mentioned this citizenship exactly one beating and one painful night in the stocks ago. As with the slave girl situation, we're left to guess at Paul's timing, but once he discloses his citizenship, things immediately change. The officials know Paul could make a stink about how they treated him and that if he does, they'll be in a world of hurt with their supervisors. They beg him to leave and not make a scene. He does, and he and Silas move on to the next town, Thessalonica. It's in this town that we hear anastatoo once again.

Paul and Silas are only in Thessalonica for three weeks and already their work is causing economic disruption in the town. In a situation similar to the tensions in Philippi, the wealthy and powerful citizens of Thessalonica make false accusations and get people all riled up. A mob forms. Mobs make a tremendous amount of noise, with all sorts of rumbling and yelling. You'd think in the din it would be hard to hear much of anything with precision. But out of all the noise, one accusation stands out enough to have been recorded. That accusation has the word "anastatoo" in it. We read it in Acts 17:6 (New King James Version), "These who have turned the world UPSIDEDOWN have come here too."

Paul and Silas never get to respond to this accusation, since they are hiding. Their friends have hidden them and manage to sneak them out of the city without being seen. So the story as we have it is limited in its details, but the accusation still gives us much to think about.

Say they weren't able to sneak out of the city. Instead, imagine they were arrested, because this time Silas isn't going to wait to see what Paul's strategy is. Silas doesn't want the tar beaten out of him again or to spend the night in jail, or worse, so he immediately yells out that Paul is a Roman citizen! This means they stand trial.

Let's consider how a trial might unfold. What would they say in their defence? What exactly would their accusers point to as evidence of turning the world UPSIDEDOWN? Who would the various witnesses be? Let's imagine a modern-day court scenario to help us learn more about anastatoo.

Lydia is called to the stand. She confidently takes her place beside the judge in her business casual ensemble. Her BMW 3 series is parked beside the courthouse. She started the morning with some yoga and a healthy breakfast. We know this because she took a picture of her bowl of granola, yogurt, and turmeric for Instagram. Later tonight she has her book club. While on the stand, she tells her story in a manner predictable, given her age, stage, and wage. She shares that despite her life matching up well with the stylized media portrayal of the ideal life, she felt incomplete. She tells the court how she had recently decided to explore her spiritual side in more depth to see if she might address this emptiness. After trying a few different churches, she heard about a group that met on the riverbank. She loves nature, so she decided to go check it out. She liked it and went back. The third time she was there, Paul and Silas showed up, and she loved what they had to say. She accepted their teachings and gave them a place to stay. She has never felt happier or more fulfilled. They helped her find the God she was longing for.

The judge is confused. Her testimony is more a spiritual testimony than a legal one. Her testimony isn't enough to convict anyone of anything. Hardly even pertinent to the revolutionary charges. He gets a bit testy!

"Counsellor, quit wasting the court's time! Call your next witness."

"Sorry, Your Honour. I call Madison Wilson to the stand."

The formerly demon-possessed slave girl takes the stand. I've decided to call her "Madison Wilson" because she deserves a better name than "demon-possessed slave girl." The prosecuting attorney starts in on Madison, imagining a vulnerable shell of a girl being steered easily to his desired end. He has grilled people on the stand who have been trafficked before, and they're easily flustered. It doesn't happen. She's confident and her story is inspiring. She enrolled in college. Her tuition is paid by the local church. She rents a room at Lydia's house, the same one Paul and Silas stayed in. She's dating the jailer's son, a fine young man with the nicest blue eyes. The judge feels like he has found himself in the middle of the sort of corny movie his wife likes, and in a patronizing way peers over his glasses at the sweating attorney.

"Counsellor, I fail to see how this witness has any relevance to the charges of turning the world UPSIDEDOWN. Do you have any more witnesses to call?"

He does. He has two more. He's tempted to skip the jailer and go right to the slave owners, since the first two witnesses weren't much help. What the heck? It can't get any worse.

"Yes, Your Honour, I do."

The judge invites the jailer to the front, and before the six-feet-two-inches of lanky redneck swagger can even slide into the witness chair, the prosecutor knows he has made a mistake. The jailer wore his old army uniform. There are medals on the front. He looks like a hero—a hero who's already fed up with this bureaucratic nonsense. The prosecutor stands up and starts to ask a question, but the jailer ignores him and turns to the judge.

"Your Honour, I don't know about this whole UPSIDEDOWN thing."

He pauses to spit out some tobacco, possibly hitting the prosecutor's shoe.

"But what I do know is that I was about to kill myself, and they stopped me. They had no reason to. I had beaten them up good. I used to get carried away with that sort of thing, but not anymore. I haven't hit anyone since I met these two. Plus, I don't have scary nightmares anymore."

When he says this last line, he looks like an innocent ten-year-old instead of a man who has killed and tortured others for the last twenty years. It takes the judge a moment to get his bearings. The judge has nightmares of his own. He dismisses the witness.

The last witnesses are the only ones we can imagine being remotely helpful for the prosecution. They accuse Paul and Silas in court like they did on the street. They say, "These men were teaching customs that are illegal for us Romans to practise." But their story is unconvincing. They're forced to appeal to patriotism, because they can't jolly well say, "These men have restored peace and mental health to a young woman, and it's costing us money!" You don't sway the judge that way. You appeal to the judge with custom, religion, and national pride to disguise your greedy motivation. Use inflammatory words like "anastatoo," add a little down-home southern charm, and the judge will be eating out of the palm of your hand. If you doubt me, read any John Grisham novel.

The prosecutor is left with not much of a case. There is no visible revolution, no army, no overt threat—really nothing that could stand up in court. The judge throws the case out and everyone celebrates. In the movie version, the jailer's son proposes to Madison. Paul and Silas beam like proud uncles as she agrees to marry him. The early strains of Steve Winwood's "Back in the High Life Again" begin to swell as the whole Philippi crew, minus the slave owners, walk hand in hand down the courtroom steps. Justice is served! The case has been dismissed.

I believe justice was served, but I do wonder if the case against Paul and Silas wasn't a bit stronger than the judge realized. In fact, if the judge had listened more closely, he might have seen that those accusing Paul and Silas are on to something. That despite the lack of incriminating evidence, something dangerous was happening. What happens when these personal transformations ripple into society at large? Not exactly a revolution, but maybe the seeds of revolution.

Seeds are one of the analogies Jesus uses to explain what is happening here, but I'm not a gardener so I prefer one of his others. I like when he uses yeast to explain (Mt. 13). I bake bread every now and have learned the hard way about the power of yeast. It doesn't take much yeast to cause some serious changes in a large lump of dough. When the judge dismissed the case and sent everyone home, he didn't know he was putting yeast back into dough. He didn't know it was going to eventually affect the whole loaf.

Take Lydia as an example. Say one of her acquaintances was a regular customer of the enslaved psychic girl. This woman goes for her weekly appointment and sees that the slave owners have shut down the shop. She imagines she'll never see Madison again. Slaves have a way of disappearing. Imagine her surprise when she's sitting in Lydia's living room for book club and sees Madison in the kitchen making herself a sandwich. She stays after book club and bursts with questions. As Lydia shares that she's following Jesus and enjoying being filling with the Holy Spirit, her friend decides to follow Jesus as well.

Now filled with the Holy Spirit, the fear that drove her to frequent a psychic is gone. One less customer for the owners of the other establishments in town offering similar services. There's nothing revolutionary happening here until you understand that this kind of scenario is going to unfold one hundred times. Maybe one thousand times. It's going to be unbelievably bad for business. The economy of the town is turned UPSIDEDOWN.

We could play out a similar scenario with the jailer. He never took the military up on their offer of free counselling for veterans. While many have dealt with PTSD—thanks to their own courage, the support of their loved ones, and the work of gifted counsellors—our jailer was not one of those. He wasn't interested in sitting on a couch for an hour a week to talk "fluff" with a shrink who had never worked a day in his life. There were better options for numbing the pain. But now, the cash he used to spend at the brothel, the arena, or the bar isn't flowing in those directions. As the Holy Spirit heals him of his emotional trauma, he focuses his money and time in other directions. This means one fewer customer at the bar, one fewer ticket sold to the gladiators, and one fewer man buying sex.

The Holy Spirit gives him the courage he needs to sit with a counsellor. Over time, his powerful personal transformation turns into a social revolution. Broken men find wholeness as he tells his story. Husbands and fathers start getting their act together. It starts small, but how many years and generations before you could call it a revolution? Ten years? Twenty-five years? How long does it take to change a family tree?

What about the conditions in the jail? Those can change pretty quickly. There are, no doubt, orders the jailer must follow. But there are many ways a "Christian" jailer can ease the suffering and preserve the dignity of prisoners and still perform those duties. Consider Paul and Silas's placement in stocks in the middle of the jail. This was not for security reasons. Stocks are an instrument of torture, forcing the victim into an uncomfortable position with zero mobility. Twenty minutes in such a device would hurt; hours would agonize. If you've been beaten previously, as Paul and

Silas were, you get locked in place already sporting a brutal injury. Do you already have a separated shoulder, a bruised tailbone, a bare back shred to ribbons? And what happens when you have to go to the bathroom?

We don't imagine a Christian jailer being able to turn the jail into a five or even two-star hotel with a breakfast buffet, but we do imagine him no longer having the taste for cruelty he once had. Does a Christian jailer not bother with stocks? Does he use chains that allow for mobility or bathroom breaks? Does he dress the wounds of the prisoners?

He isn't in a place of power where he can reform the entire Roman penal system, but he can be yeast. As anyone who has worked with a variety of supervisors knows, the same shift can feel vastly different depending on the boss. This is true even when both supervisors have the same handbook guiding them, because if one follows Jesus, the handbook plays out differently. The accusations about turning the world UPSIDEDOWN might be less exaggerated than they seem.

Anastatoo and You

Clearly, we've wandered into historical fiction. The specifics about Lydia, Madison, and the jailer are all made up. We don't know what happened to each of them, but we know that if they continued to follow Jesus, they would eventually change the composition of the world around them, because this is what yeast does. Each of them, because they now follow Jesus, are going to bring just the right amount and kind of anastatoo. They each will turn things UPSIDEDOWN in their spheres of influence.

So will you.

Your transformation will lead to social revolution. Your healing will have ripple effects and fix what is broken around you. This is eventually how God's UPSIDEDOWN dream comes true. It's a brilliant plan. He leverages how many of us there are and how unique each of us is. We work away as yeast in the various loaves we find ourselves in and become the people who are turning the world UPSIDEDOWN. I say the "the loaves we find ourselves in" to illustrate how different each loaf might be and how strategic Jesus is when he leverages our diversity.

The jailer and Lydia may never once be in the same social circle. He isn't going to be a guest at her book club, and she isn't going to go to his UFC party. Different ages, stages, and wages. All people, having been met powerfully by Jesus, are now turning the world UPSIDEDOWN in a way unique to each of them in a sphere of influence assigned to each of them. They're not becoming clones. Remember the hybrid idea from the first chapter? This is what's happening. They're becoming more like Jesus, yes, but also more like their true selves. They fix the world as they become what they were meant to be. The possibilities are beautiful to imagine.

Perhaps her sensitivity to the spiritual realm, now having been redeemed, allows our former slave girl to become a gifted teacher or worship leader.

Perhaps materialistic Lydia stops worrying about being rich and repositions her garment company as an ethically sourced cooperative.

Maybe the jailer's unique past opens doors to retired soldiers who have become decision-making politicians, and he becomes surprisingly influential as a down-to-earth lobbyist.

Notice how in these examples what was maybe the worst parts of their lives end up being the parts Jesus especially uses to help other people? We just came full circle on the clone/hybrid idea, and now we round out the "edible puzzles" one. Jesus uses your ingredients and adds his to make something wonderful. I wonder what it will look like for you? There are as many ways to turn the world UPSIDEDOWN as there are followers of Jesus. You don't have to do anything special to make your own unique contribution toward achieving the UPSIDEDOWN dream. You just bring your ingredients and give consent to Jesus. You'll be surprised what he uses. He won't throw away some of what you imagine he might. He doesn't discard our broken uniqueness. He redeems it.

Consider a few modern examples of how this might look for you. First, consider pornography. Someone who chooses to follow Jesus and has God's UPSIDEDOWN dream in view will soon be asked by Jesus to stop using pornography. Through the power of the Holy Spirit and the power of their Christian community, he will be able to do this. Once he has, he'll feel lightness, purity, and freedom that he forgot was possible for a human being to feel. It will feel good. As British comedian Russell Brand puts it: "No one closes their laptop after wanking off and says to themselves, 'Now that is what I was put on the planet to do.'" Ahh Russell, the next logical career step for you is seminary. I can get you in; it will be fun. We can turn it into a movie. It can be a sequel to *Get Him to the Greek*, although I'd like to be played by a different actor than Jonah Hill.

Russell Brand is right. The general feelings associated with "wanking off" are loneliness, incompleteness, and compromise. Since intimacy, wholeness, and gratitude are serious upgrades, I have yet to meet someone who has kicked a pornography addiction and misses the "good old days."

But it isn't enough for the Christian to stop using. Now he feels compelled to do something about it. Since the objectification, the loss of personal control, the lack of intimacy, and the contempt that go hand in hand with pornography are all directly opposed to the path of Jesus, he can't be content with mere personal freedom. His personal freedom must ripple. The yeast must ferment. He can't sit idly by as pornography provides fuel for sex trafficking and slavery. It isn't enough for him to be safe, secure, and healthy personally; because he's following Jesus, he's compelled to help people who need help.

So he donates to an anti-slavery group. He redoes the siding at a women's shelter for free. He boycotts hotels that have no Wi-Fi filter. His social media posts raise awareness that pornography is something sinister, that underneath the veneer of freedom of expression, millions of people are enslaved in one way or another. Soon he's fighting a multi-billion-dollar industry in ways he never would have imagined. His personal transformation and God's dream compels him. Certainly, like Paul and Silas, he will meet resistance as his values of justice and mercy crash into the values of power and money. And like the slave owners, modern people who make money off human suffering will reframe their desire for power and money as the protection of liberty and freedom. There's always opposition at the place where God's UPSIDEDOWN dream crashes into the status quo, but living at that intersection is what it means to be Christian, and it's more fulfilling than buy-one-get-one-free Kirkland cashews.

If it's hard to imagine yourself as a global crusader for human rights, it doesn't mean your life will be any less revolutionary. It just might be more subtle. Many habits and cultural norms disguise and normalize an ugliness that doesn't become visible until someone begins to follow

Jesus. For example, it's assumed that people will complain and gossip. An embarrassingly high percentage of daily conversation is spent this way. Frequently, this gossip becomes objectifying or dehumanizing. It usually involves someone expressing contempt—haughty sniffs through the nose, shaking the head in disgust, and long eye rolls. These behaviours are something those who follow Jesus have been helped by the Holy Spirit to stop doing. Contempt is dangerous because it stops you from seeing the value inherent in people. Once you have contempt in your heart, you can justify nearly any kind of mistreatment of those you find contemptible. Christians have a zero-contempt policy. Having contempt is logically impossible for someone who follows Jesus, because Jesus believes everyone has the breath of God in them and is automatically valuable beyond comprehension.

So as a Christian, you stop talking and acting with contempt. This might take the form of you refusing to chime in when the boss is being decimated behind her back in the staff room, or when you don't join in with the guys as they evaluate the anatomy of the young woman who served you lunch, or when you don't help your jealous friends minimize the achievements or possessions of a wealthy acquaintance. It might seem small, but the absence of contempt is revolutionary. Contempt is such an accepted part of daily life that people notice the absence of it almost immediately.

When people see you refuse to talk and act with contempt, they will change how they talk and act around you. Some are glad for the change. You're calling them to become a better version of themselves. Some get annoyed, also because you're calling them to become a better version of themselves. But whether people like it or hate it, you are changing things. You're turning the world UPSIDEDOWN. There are no riots. No one throwing you into jail. But you are revolutionary because you're refusing to engage in any conversation poisoned with toxic contempt. You're nudging the world "as it is" in the direction of the world God is dreaming about.

A few years ago, a couple new to our church joined the weekly small group that met in our house. About three months in, I asked them to share their early experiences of the group. They said there was something that shocked them about our group. I got a tad worried. I wasn't fishing for anything shocking. But it was OK. What shocked them was the lack of complaining and gossiping. They had never been with people who didn't spend the bulk of their time together this way. They didn't know people could get together and be this positive. Most of their social circles, and even their family situations, had been master classes on ruining the reputations of people not in the room. They loved the absence of contempt in our group. They were going to be like that. They were going to give their kids the gift of parents who weren't always talking about how miserable everything, and everyone, is. Family trees were going to change. Lack of contempt is revolutionary.

This contempt example is less sensational than the pornography one, but don't imagine it's any less potent. Consider how contempt for others lies at the root of most human cruelty. Is there theft without contempt? Is there spousal abuse without contempt? Is there sexual harassment without contempt? Is there slavery without contempt? No. And, of course, a world without contempt also makes pornography and sex trafficking impossible. Both require devaluing others enough that we feel OK treating them in ways we wouldn't want to be treated.

When you cease to add any fuel to contempt's fire, when you intentionally douse the fire, you're being revolutionary. This is no exaggeration. You have marched in no protest. You haven't been involved in politics at all. No jury would convict you. How could they? You just had people at your house for two hours every week for a month and didn't gossip or complain, and now their family is forever transformed and different. Jesus has changed how you speak and think, and the ripple effects are revolutionary. And that's just with contempt! Think of all the other places your transformation will cause revolution.

Imagine the ripple effects when you cease to worry about your reputation. Free from having to manipulate how people see you, you can be present with people and not perform for them. You begin to really know others and feel known. Also, since you're no longer managing your image, you're free to include those who don't enhance it in the eyes of others. You become the cure for loneliness for the isolated and neglected around you. You may never know how many people your inclusive heart saved from suicide, but you can bet there will be more than one life you save over the course of your lifetime.

Or maybe the worry is financial security. Now freed by Jesus from the anxiety of wondering if you'll have enough, you're free to give generously to support causes that matter. The hungry are fed. Those struggling with mental illness are protected. The homeless have shelter. The sick can afford medicine. And because the joy of using money to bless people far eclipses the joy of counting and spending it, your penny-pinching peers see a radiance on your face they don't see in the mirror. You challenge and inspire them to bless others with their plenty. Both those in need and those who have much lead happier lives because of your worry-free generosity.

Crazy ripple effects, huh? And that's just contempt and worry. We haven't even started to imagine what happens when you become less jealous, angry, judging, or tired. Nor will we. You get the point. God's brilliant plan for achieving his UPSIDEDOWN dream is to cover the globe with people who are being transformed as they follow Jesus. The ripple effects of that transformation will spread through history and geography until the earth is as God wants it to be, until his UPSIDEDOWN dream comes true.

What the Dream Is NOT

You are a relatively new Christian, so maybe you haven't noticed that we're well into describing God's UPSIDEDOWN dream and haven't yet hinted at what many Christians assume God's dream is. Specifically, we haven't talked once about going to heaven when you die. The reason we haven't talked about it is simple. God doesn't dream about getting you into heaven. He has something else on his mind.

He dreams of bringing heaven to planet Earth. His dream isn't the extraction of Christians from the earth. It's not of removing the yeast from the dough but of it working its way through the entire loaf. He doesn't dream of people going to heaven when they die but of a redeemed human race delighting in their existence in a newly renovated heaven and earth. These are the things God dreams of, and it's a fatal misunderstanding to think otherwise.

Fatal because to see God's dream as helping followers of Jesus escape from earth turns it into a nightmare. History tells this nightmarish story where the end (getting to heaven) justifies the means (whatever it takes). Look at the places in the past where securing access to heaven became the number one priority for Christians and you'll see those incidents and eras that are most regrettable and shameful. Places where current human suffering was condoned because of the promise of relief in the afterlife. Places where the environment was abused because this world is "not my home, I'm just passing through." Places where cultural genocide was permitted because the overarching goal, captured succinctly and specifically in U.S. Army Capt. Richard Pratt's 1892 speech, was to "kill the Indian, and save the man."

All these tragedies linked to the belief that God dreams of extracting us. But he doesn't dream of extraction, he dreams of empowerment and transformation. When you see this, when you see God dreams of bringing heaven to planet Earth, instead of getting Christians to heaven, everything shifts. Perhaps the most meaningful practical shift is this: Christians have to put our grubby paws back on the world. The extraction mistake encourages us to think that if we're going to be taken away from all this eventually, we may as well get a head start. It's the extraction version of the story that makes sense of an isolated Christian subculture. Christian radio. Christian fiction. Christian movies. Christian schools. All designed to create a sort of bubble where we can avoid contagion until Jesus gets us out of here

I won't spend any more time on this. The UPSIDEDOWN dream exposes this as harmful nonsense. We are not to avoid contagion. We are to be contagious. We are not to ignore the damaging patterns and habits around us. We are to disrupt them and bring something better. We don't take our hands off the world around us to stay pure. We lay hands on the world to hold it, shape it, and bless it. You don't get accused of anastatoo if your end game is to go to heaven when you die.

This chapter has been exciting. I don't imagine you'll sleep a wink tonight as you imagine all the ripple effects your pursuit of the UPSIDEDOWN dream will have. Imagine what lies ahead for you. Will you baptize an abusive jailer in the wee hours of the morning? Will you know the proper moment to disclose your true citizenship? Will you find a sugar momma down by the river? These are important questions, and it's no wonder you can't sleep. But now I can't sleep, because if these are the questions you're asking, then I have failed you.

With this sense of failure, I would go to my wife for comfort and find none. She would agree that I have failed you. She would see three failures. First, she'd point out that I am lying to you, because even though I told you I can't sleep, I can. In her words, I sleep like a mildly concussed baby. She probably doesn't remember saying that.

The second point of failure she'd see is every attempt I've made at humour. I know at this stage, faithful reader, you have tremendous affection for me, delight in my whimsy, and might want to leap to my defence, but that is unnecessary. When she persecutes me like this, I just remind her I am a Canadian citizen, and she backs off. Plus, she looks so darn cute and sexy when she's giving critical assessments that I am OK with it.

Her third criticism would be that I've been too theoretical. People need next steps, practical things to do! They need a specific path to follow. She'd get quite animated on point number three; her volume would increase and her index finger would jab me in the ribs to make sure I'm paying attention. I am paying attention. You can tell because of how I'm giggling. I'd give her a wink and a "I hear you, baby!" This makes it seem like I'm not taking her as seriously as she'd like, but deep down I know swaggering confidence is necessary to shift this from a "feedback" session to something with a little more candlelight and a lot more tenderness. Want me to give practical steps, eh? Let the reader watch and learn as I turn criticism into foreplay.

Tamara is not in the room with me right now, but I suspect she will burst in shortly with a sense that I'm up to something. I don't think I'll show her the last few paragraphs. And sure enough, no word of a lie, she just walked into my office here at work as I wrote this paragraph. I took the opportunity to read to her what I just wrote. She expressed strong feelings.

Lest you think I'm being cavalier about any failings, or that I don't listen to feedback, I do agree with her last criticism. We need some practical steps. Her criticism is not wrong, only premature. I'll thank you, Tamara Lynn Weselake, to reserve judgment until you read the book in its entirety.

We still have Part Three to go, where I intend to right every wrong committed thus far. It's about to get pragmatic and intentional. But for now, why don't I slip into something a little more comfortable?

Where are you going?

Come back.

Sigh.

CHAPTER 3

From UPSIDEDOWN to UP SIDE DOWN

Come join me in a first-year Bible college class. I saved you a chair. The class is "Principles of Exegesis 1: Rise of the Exegetes."

The dashing young professor strides to the whiteboard and writes, "God is nowhere!" in a crisp 108-point Cambrian font and then turns and smiles, mischievous dimples all over the place. Take a quick look around the room and you'll see that the professor has caused exactly the reaction he wanted to. See the studious types raise their eyebrows and then have to push their glasses back up their nose. You can almost hear their frantic inner monologue (*Don't use your middle finger, Leroy. Not the middle finger. This is freshman Bible college course and a chance to re-invent yourself. No one knows what a nerd you were back at Leland High School. Show them you are one worldly streetwise cool cat. Push those glasses up with your index finger, like it's the most natural thing in the world.*) Feel the cold panic in the room as the homeschooled kids realize that their parents' fears of "book learning" are well-founded. Notice the intentional shift in posture as a growing number of young women realize the young professor isn't wearing a wedding ring. Get caught up in the anticipation as he turns back toward the board and writes again.

When you see what he writes next, it hits you hard enough to nearly knock you out of your chair—a chair you're finding most uncomfortable due to the little plaque screwed to its seat acknowledging the generosity

51

of the class of 1984. You stay seated, but barely, because underneath the previous statement declaring the absolute absence of God this brilliant man has now, simply by changing the spacing of what he first wrote, changed everything:

"God is now here!"

It's like the same letters, but the opposite meaning!

You are totally impressed but don't want to let it show. You're already finding it hard not to resent Professor Studly. When the competition for female attention was Leroy, you liked your chances, but in the last few minutes, you've seen your odds of dating one of these girls take a serious hit as they compare your modest freshman intellect, weak jaw, and scrawny calves to this complex, dashing mental dynamo with the class in the palm of his hand. He knows he is THAT good. You know he is THAT good. Would you date yourself after seeing that there are guys like this out there? Not a chance.

Professor Studly pivots a slow turn back toward the class and offers a smirk. Did you imagine he just made eye contact with arguably the three most attractive students in class? Based on their crimson cheeks and the way they're fanning themselves with their notebooks, it seems like they noticed. You are annoyed! Who does this guy think he is?

And he isn't done! He's back at the board writing:

"Did you ever see a bun dance on the table?"

What? Despite your annoyance, you're intrigued. What is he up to? After a deliberate delay, more eye contact, and a tight pirouette, he writes again:

"Did you ever see abundance on the table?"

OK. This time your jealousy isn't so strong to stop you from joining in the applause. You've never seen such brilliance. You never imagined such intellectual insight and animal magnetism could exist in one package. You admit defeat to the alpha male in the room.

He has you intrigued. This is what it means to study scripture—to look and look again! To realize, at first glance, that it reads "God is nowhere!" But then, instead of panicking, to have the discipline to keep digging, to chip away at the text until you realize your mistake and sigh with relief. To be confused by dancing buns and then to have it clarified that buns were never dancing in the first place. You're going to enjoy "Principles of Exegesis 1: Rise of the Exegetes." Although hopefully he explains what "exegesis" means at some point, because right now you have no clue.

Just in case Professor Studly takes a while to get to it, Uncle Nathan will explain. Exegesis is a technical word to do with interpreting scripture. Exegesis is what you do when you're trying to understand the intentions of the author and the level of understanding of the original audience. You do this so you can better understand the Bible.

Someone who is performing exegesis (an exegete) is asking all sorts of questions that take her beyond a surface reading of a text. Questions like: What was happening at the time? How were these words being used at that time in history? What social or economic factors would have shaped how people heard this? Is this an urban or rural perspective? What is the author's agenda? Why might she have that agenda? What is the genre? Is this a poem? A recipe? A memoir? The more we ask questions like these, the closer we get to proper understanding.

We can use Professor Studly's examples to see how this works. We assume the ancient words on the old manuscript are blurred together enough to have made it impossible to know just by looking if we should read "God is now here!" or "God is nowhere." But we can still figure it out. If the phrase is in the middle of a celebration of thanksgiving, we have a strong clue that the best interpretation is "God is now here!" If the context is Israel conquered and enslaved, then the more pessimistic lament of "God is nowhere!" would appear to be a better understanding.

But we can't yet be sure. Often there is nuance that isn't seen at first glance. Take the first example. Even though the phrase occurs in the middle of a celebration, and it seems natural that the author would be celebrating the presence of God, perhaps she has other intentions. Perhaps she wants to warn a complacent Israel that their celebrations keep them from noticing that God has abandoned them, that in the midst of their revelry she's telling them to sober up, look around, and notice—God is nowhere to be found.

We see the same potential in the second example. When we take into account intention as well as context, we see the author is encouraging the slaves that, despite their lot, God has not abandoned them. Yes, they are exiled in a foreign city and far from the familiar temples and rituals they associate with God, but take heart! God is now here!

One of the classic goals of exegesis is to ensure a passage of scripture means the same thing to you as it did to the original audience. One of my decidedly unsexy professor's mantras was "It can't mean something different to you than it did to them." This makes sense. If we don't understand the intention or original context, we simply project our desired meaning to the text and make it mean what we want it to mean. When we do this, the Bible loses its potency to transform us. It can't critique us or inform our actions, because we make it mean what we want it to mean. We treat it as a screen on which to project our ideas and longings instead of a projector that sheds light on our lives. We see what we want to see. We use the Bible to make our point instead of having it shape us, and we're left only with "what this verse means to me" subjectivity. This erodes the value of scripture. Exegesis saves us from this predicament, a predicament all too easy to fall into.

When I was twenty years old, I was invited to move to Austin, Texas, and be a part of starting a church. I needed to secure almost $25k a year, for four years, in US dollars to do this. This was a daunting task, made worse by the fact that most of my funding would come from Canadian wallets, and the Canadian dollar was worth only seventy cents US. I needed to pull out all the stops. I needed to write the greatest fundraising letter of all time. I scoured the Bible for the most inspiring lines I could find and finally settled on this:

"Look around at the nations; look and be amazed. For I am doing something in your own day, something you wouldn't believe even if someone told you about it." (Habakkuk 1:5 New Living Translation)

That's the sort of thing that gets Christians writing cheques, baby! You are probably fighting an urge to send me money just based on that verse. I tagged this inspiring line onto both the top and bottom of the letter. I was hoping people would see it as an official biblical validation of the exceedingly great things God had personally called me to—sort of like company letterhead validates a memo. I was surging with confidence as I prepared these letters. I promised God I would buy my dad a truck if I received in excess of $100k.

My optimism was misplaced. No money was donated. To be fair, this is because I never did send out the letter. Some major early partners I thought would support me backed out and effectively put a stop to my plans. This was sad for me, but the upside was that I didn't send out 100-plus fundraising letters with horrible exegesis. My brilliant vision casting line? Turned out to be about coming carnage and pain.

If I had been curious about those amazing things God had in store in Habakkuk, I could have kept reading and found threats like "I [God] am going to send the Babylonians to destroy you and punish you." Not the most inspiring, although perhaps I might have scared people into donating. It turns out Habakkuk isn't writing a fundraising letter. He's sending a dire warning, and the original audience catch what he is pitching. But not me. I took it 100 per cent out of context to make my own point. This might seem like a relatively harmless situation, but you don't have to be a Christian for long to see much more serious and painful examples of what can happen when people use the Bible to serve their own ends.

But you haven't been a Christian for long, so I'll list a few consequences of crummy exegesis for you that I have seen. Where there is poor exegesis: Women are marginalized. Slavery is validated. Wonky end-time escapist scenarios rob people of joy and meaning. Violence is permitted. Injustice is ignored. Wealth is seen as a divine blessing. Poverty as divine punishment. God is angry 24/7. Indeed, much of what mainstream culture is suspicious of in Christian culture are the parts of Christian culture that are due to terrible exegesis. This is unfortunate but easy enough to fix with better exegesis.

Better exegesis is what we've been doing this whole time. What? Yes! It is true. Solid exegesis, and worthy of an A+ from our sexy prof. Although now he might be so threatened by us that it's hard for him to reward us properly. Jealousy will do that, and we're no longer even in the same league as that amateur trying to impress with buns dancing on tables and "God is now here/God is nowhere" distinctions. The pupils are outshining the teacher. When the jealous and petty prof gives us an F on our paper, we might need to go to the academic dean, who will see the brilliance of our exegesis and recommend we continue to do PhD work. Then the comely coeds will see the error of their ways and line up to dance with us at the college toga parties.

And what exactly is this exegesis I'm so proud of? Our genius level exegesis, or "exegenius" if you prefer the dad joke version, is demonstrated by our use of the phrase "God's UPSIDEDOWN dream." If it's not immediately apparent why we will be receiving scholarships to Yale Divinity School based on this alone, allow me to elaborate. Earlier, I mentioned I was sheepish about using anastatoo as a central concept in this book when it's only used three times in the Bible, but I was pretending. I was bluffing. I wasn't the least bit sheepish. This is because anastatoo helps us rightfully interpret one the central concepts in the Bible—the Kingdom of God.

There are many ways we could back up the claim that the Kingdom of God is central, but the most convincing support comes when you realize that nearly every time Jesus opens his mouth, he's talking about it. This is easy enough to establish. Read his words and you'll see it to be the case. What's harder to understand is what he has in mind when he talks about "the Kingdom of God." This is where diligent exegesis helps, as it considers each place the phrase is used, the larger context of the setting, the ways similar phases were being used in that era, the way the earliest listeners seemed to understand the phrase, and the behaviour of those who accepted Jesus's teachings about the Kingdom of God. As we put together the exegesis clues, we find that they lead us to anastatoo and eventually to the conclusion that the phrase "God's UPSIDEDOWN dream" is a great way to interpret what Jesus meant when he said, "Kingdom of God."

You'll see how well this works when we swap out the phrase "Kingdom of God" for "God's UPSIDEDOWN dream" in Jesus's sermons. Consider this snippet inspired by the parables in Matthew 13:

God's UPSIDEDOWN dream is like a farmer scattering seeds. Some lands on rocky soil. Some is choked out by weeds. And some grow to maturity and produce an exponential amount of fruit.

Now how about this familiar example from The Lord's Prayer:

Father in heaven. Holy is your name. May your UPSIDEDOWN dreams for planet Earth come true.

Or this beautiful idea from Mark 19:14:

Let the little children come to me, because they are the primary beneficiaries of God's UPSIDEDOWN dream.

That swap works pretty well, doesn't it? It turns out that God's UPSIDEDOWN dream illuminates a central theme in the Bible and help us understand the words on the tip of Jesus's tongue. We got to this understanding because of our exegesis. We looked at anastatoo from a few different angles. We looked at the context it was in, the behaviour of the people at the time, and the patterns of conduct. All of this served to help us get a clear understanding. Hooray for us and our exegesis!

As excited as we might be about this, we need to realize that exegesis isn't the only approach to reading and understanding the Bible. Of course, there have to be other options besides rational, deliberate, and academic exegesis, since the Bible is not a textbook. The Bible was written with passion by mystical people, people who often had mind-blowing spiritual experiences. Many of these people weren't worried one iota about making logical arguments, choosing just the right wording, presenting stories with consistency, or objectively describing events. The Bible is a wild book, and exegesis is the attempt to tame it. But if the Bible becomes too domesticated, it loses some of its spiritual and mystical potency. Yes, the Bible requires exegesis, but we also need to allow it to be the mysterious book that masters and moves us. We need to be open to it connecting with us in a deeper way than rational thought. The Bible speaks to our minds, but we need to move beyond exegesis and anticipate the Bible also speaking directly to our spirit.

Our spiritual connection with the Bible is facilitated by the Holy Spirit in two ways. First, the Holy Spirit was there when the words were being written. He was instrumental in how the Bible was written, compiled, and protected through the ages. The various authors of the Bible didn't write on their own but were rather co-authors with the Holy Spirit. Second, the Holy Spirit is there when the words are being read. The co-author of the book is sitting there with you when you read it. This means the Holy Spirit can illuminate for us in real time what God wants us to see in the Bible. The Spirit brings the Bible to life for us in personal ways—the Spirit knows both us and the Bible, inside and out. The Holy Spirit's intimate knowledge of both text and reader raises our expectations about what we will experience as we read the Bible. We come to it asking the Holy Spirit, "What do you have here for us today? And what personal and unique message might we receive?"

I say "personal and unique" because if I read a verse, and you read the same verse, the Holy Spirit might have it mean something to me that it doesn't mean to you. In fact, you might be the first person to be blessed, or convicted, by a passage of the Bible in that way. It's entirely possible a verse can mean something to you that it has never meant to anyone else in history, despite however many pounds of ink have been spilled by those doing thorough academic exegesis and who have arrived at nearly unanimous conclusions about what the verse technically means. Yet you found something new! This is exciting but also controversial.

Nearly two thousand years into having the Bible, is it possible to have an original experience with it? Given the millions of people through history who have read and studied it, do we think we're going to find something new? The answer is a resounding "Yes." Because of the Holy Spirit and our own individual personalities and histories, every reader comes at the text from a different angle of approach. In that way, every reader is an original reader and can expect to find something unique and fresh for themselves.

At this point, I imagine a few different reactions to what I've been saying. The more artistic or romantic reader is feeling their heart warmed as they imagine quiet early morning moments when the Holy Spirit illuminates just the right verse, at just the right time, in a way just for them. However, more academically inclined types are getting worried. The academic dean is not so supportive at this point. He has cancelled his lunch plans with us. It looks like we might not get into Yale after all. And no matter which approach you use, you can't deny that your approach seems to contradict the other. It doesn't appear to be a matter of preference. It appears to be the case that one approach has to be true and the other false.

I appreciate this dilemma. I've lived in the middle of it for decades. I received the same modern bias in my education as the academic dean did. We were taught exegesis and to be wary of the more subjective, personal approach. Since that formal education, though, I've had many personal and powerful experiences with the Bible that wouldn't hold up to the scrutiny of exegesis. But I'm not prepared to say that those weren't legitimate experiences simply because they weren't rational. Nor am I willing to entirely untether myself from the wisdom and guardrails of exegesis.

Let me share my attempt to hold these two approaches together. I've found it helpful to stop thinking of my goal as "trying to understand the Bible." Instead, I position myself to try to hear a voice. Obviously, to properly hear a voice means comprehending what that voice is saying. When we nod our heads and say, "I hear you!" we don't mean that we hear only the sound of their voice but that we're also catching the meaning. Part of hearing a voice means understanding the words the person is speaking.

But hearing a voice also involves something more than comprehending the words being used. It also involves paying attention to body language, tone, and even the current state of the relationship we have with the person speaking to us. Unless we have these other factors on our radar, we may not properly hear what's being said. We've all had moments when we misinterpreted what someone meant because we chose to focus only on what they said and not how they said it. Had we paid attention to tone or looked them in the eyes as they were talking or remembered a shared experience, we would have caught their intended meaning. But we focused solely on the words they used and didn't actually hear them; we missed their voice.

Everyone has experienced this first-hand, and it probably sounded like this:

Nathan, stubbornly: "But you said . . ."

Tamara, with a sigh: "Yes . . . but what I meant was . . ."

And the truth is, if I had paid attention to what her body language was saying, I'd have understood her meaning. If I had noticed the tear, or twinkle, in her eye, I'd have gotten it. To understand requires more than attention to words—it requires a broader attentiveness. To hear someone clearly requires paying attention to their head and their heart.

Most of us will gravitate to one way of reading the Bible; we'll lean toward either the heart or the head. Whichever way you lean, try to find a balance. Don't worry about nailing the exact balance, but you ought to make both approaches part of your Bible reading.

You will need to use your head. Scripture is a complex ancient book written over the span of thousands of years and requires careful study to understand in depth. You will need to do research and think carefully. You will be confused by a passage that seems misogynist, sexist, or even counter to some of the teachings of Jesus. You will need to dive into the geography, politics, and social climate of the time the text was written in to understand it more clearly. Your exegetical work will keep you from including dire predictions in your fundraising letter, or sexist behaviour, as you adjust for history and social climate. You'll heave a sigh of relief that you didn't embarrass yourself, and you'll feel solid ground under your feet because you understand something in depth.

Other times, you will need your heart. The Bible is also a love letter written to you. You don't read a love letter and run it past fact checkers. That would ruin it. You don't worry about grammar or inconsistency. Who cares if they spelled "pistol whip" wrong (Tam sends me some wacky love letters), because you hear the voice of your loved one in it. You feel their nearness. You feel longing to be even nearer. As you are reading it, you hear their voice. It is worth noting I first came across this love letter idea in the writings of Søren Kierkegaard. This nineteenth-century genius was surely one of Christianity's most intellectual giants. I love that he dignifies the role of the heart when it comes to hearing God's voice. I loved it so much, I named my son after him.

Don't apologize for using your heart. Too often Christians are sheepish about what they personally glean from the Bible. Before they share how a verse encouraged them, they'll give a disclaimer like, "I know this verse probably doesn't mean this, but when I read it this morning, I felt like God was telling me he sees what I'm going through with my alienated sister." This is so good! When it happens, celebrate. You are learning to recognize God's voice.

You are also learning how closely God must be paying attention to you to be able to give you such a personal message. God paying attention to individual people is what frequently blew the minds of the people who wrote the Bible and the characters in the Bible. Let it blow yours. Since the Bible was written by people who met God, and is about people who met God, when you read it expecting to meet God, you're only taking genre into account. They wrote about and experienced a God of love. You are approaching the Bible as a love letter. Maybe using the heart doesn't mean leaving exegesis behind. Maybe it means getting better at it as we recognize the genre of love letter.

My Love Letter

Fifteen years ago, I was thinking of a mission statement for our church. If you aren't familiar with contemporary church leadership, this might seem odd. People imagine pastors as humble country pastors inhabiting an 1850s world. They help with the threshing at harvest, deliver babies, and moonlight as the local sheriff. You can spot the local minister because he's the only one who has to keep his shirt on out in the field. Poor Pastor Ray. All the other men standing around with their sweat evaporating off their bare torsos. He has to sweat like a hog through his black clergy attire. Although not for long, because a chuckwagon has just come bouncing into the field to hustle him off to the Shillington homestead. Young Ms. Shillington's baby is breech, and only his little, soft pastor hands can do what is necessary to save both child and mother.

We've gotten a little technical the last few pages and haven't had much silliness since we were enjoying Professor Studly's shenanigans. Let's relax a bit and take a little detour. It's no doubt a bit self-indulgent because I love babies and I love chuckwagons. I also love the idea of me flying into an obstetrics ward, calmly and quickly rolling up my sleeves with a commanding "Stand aside, I will deliver this baby!" Just my presence is enough to calm a panicky first-time mother and her useless and nauseous husband. Huge sighs of relief all around: "Pastor Nathan is here." And then, with the baby tucked safely in Mom's arms, and Dad's colour returning, they wave me over. They've been talking just now and decided they would like to name the baby "Nathan." I gasp. My aw shucks smile and raised eyebrows indicate a delighted surprise, but I am not surprised. This happens often, sometimes even when the child is female.

Sadly, I missed the humble country-parson era, where helping with harvest, delivering babies, and doubling as the town sheriff were all part of the job. No, I happened to be a pastor in the season of church history where pastors come up with mission statements for their church. Instead of dealing with panicking chuckwagon drivers worrying about getting to the Shillington place in time, pastors now have to deal with panicking elders worrying that mission statements are too vague.

Vagueness is a common concern with mission statements. Although, in my specific case, vagueness was not the main concern for our church board members. Their main concern was that our mission statement kept changing. One month I'd declare we were all about inviting our friends to church. The next month I'd let it be known we couldn't care less about getting "bums in chairs." Our mission was now the fight against childhood illiteracy. The next month we'd be raising money for wells in Indonesia. Their concern was legitimate. I was worse then, but I still have the tendency to get excited about a new concept, dive deep into it for about three months, and then move on. Case in point, this manuscript was written using three different word processing programs, three different laptops, and on three different continents. Although, it wasn't that I lost interest in Antarctica, I just got cold.

I agreed with the board that a mission statement had to have at least semi-permanence. I couldn't keep pulling the congregation in different directions all the time. They were getting dizzy; some were nauseous. But it also needed to allow for some creativity. I don't mind being focused, but I hate being stuck with something rigid. I needed to settle on something broad enough to allow for individual creativity so I didn't go nuts but specific enough to allow for group mobilization. Finally, it had to be simple. I wanted a five-year-old to understand. Not a genius five-year-old, like your overachieving kid. But more a dim bulb, like my five-year-old Cousin Aaron was. It couldn't be wordy. Pictures would be helpful.

I was pleased to see UPSIDEDOWN checked in all the boxes for what we needed in a mission statement. UPSIDEDOWN isn't just a description of the kind of dream God has. It also provides direction. UPSIDEDOWN doesn't just show us *what* is going to happen but *how* it's supposed to happen. It's not just about destination; it's about the path you walk to get there. It doesn't merely give us information. It gives us direction. As we will see, UPSIDEDOWN is both a description of God's dream for planet Earth and the specific mission guide for how to live in a way that makes His dream come true. UPSIDEDOWN turns out to be as big as history and the cosmos but also as small as your next decision. It worked perfectly as mission statement.

It's also a perfect example of the "love letter" category. Using strict exegesis, what I'm about to do isn't going to make sense. Exegesis gives the technical understanding of anastatoo. It explains anastatoo and allows us to reframe the concept of "the Kingdom of God" as "God's UPSIDEDOWN dream." Exegesis has shown us "what" God is wanting to have happen and what His dream is. But the love letter understanding of UPSIDEDOWN moves us beyond this. The love letter interpretation directs our path; it shows us how to pursue the UPSIDEDOWN dream. Here is how.

Instead of considering UPSIDEDOWN as two words (Upside down), as exegesis would have us do, the "love letter" approach has us consider each syllable separately: UP, SIDE, and DOWN. Where there were two words, there are now three. No textbook would ever direct you to do this, but I believe God revealed this idea to me as I prayed and meditated on scripture. This shift to considering the syllables separately was a love letter revelation.

I want to make sure you are tracking the shift from UPSIDEDOWN to UP, SIDE, and DOWN, so I'll risk over-explaining. When read this way —UPSIDEDOWN—it gives a vision of *WHAT* God's dream is for planet Earth. He wants it to be turned UPSIDEDOWN—we covered that earlier as we looked at Lydia, the demon-possessed slave girl, and the jailer. But when read as three syllables—UP, SIDE, and DOWN—it gives specific individual directions for *HOW* to do your part to make the dream a reality.

The syllables are arrows pointing you in a specific direction. Follow the UP arrow and you find yourself moving to God. The UP arrow isn't pointing to God in the sense that God is spatially located above us. Christians believe God is everywhere. The arrow is more a reminder that as we connect with him, we are elevated, and our lives ascend to something higher. Much poetry in the Bible affirms this. We were stuck in the valley, or in the muck, or in the darkness, and we called out to him. We looked to him, and he pulled us UP. Spatially and emotionally, the word works to describe how it feels when you connect with God. You are uplifted. This is the case whether you're a new believer or someone continuing to grow.

The UP syllable is about moving: **"Up to God in new and continuing relationships with Him."**

Where the UP syllable is about your relationship with God, the SIDE syllable is about human relationships. SIDE is about community. We unite on mission; we work for reconciliation; we forgive; we bear each others' burdens; we weep together; we insist on meeting together. Anything relational is a part of this syllable. Large issues, like racism, are included in the SIDE syllable. Smaller issues, like forgiving your dad, fit here too. The SIDE syllable reminds us that following Jesus isn't just a spiritual endeavour or an academic pursuit. It isn't just about personal betterment or believing the truth. The SIDE syllable reminds us that following Jesus is not a solo journey. It necessarily involves people. The side syllable is about moving: **"SIDE to each other in authentic community."**

DOWN refers to serving people and sacrificing for them. A tad more nuance required with this arrow, since there could be the misunderstanding that we are looking DOWN on those we serve in a patronizing way. But DOWN isn't about superiority; it's about humility. The syllable is about moving **"DOWN in humble acts of service."** DOWN is not the direction we look, as in "down our noses" at people. No, DOWN is the direction we move. It is the posture we take.

See how the "what" and the "how" come together?

We make the UPSIDEDOWN dream of God for planet Earth a reality as we move UP to God, SIDE to each other, and DOWN in humble acts of service.

This will naturally happen as we follow Jesus because it's what Jesus did. He made the UPSIDEDOWN dreams of God a reality by living UP, SIDE, and DOWN.

Consider: Jesus came to connect us UP to God, to make God accessible to us as our Father. He came to bring us up out of our sin and out of the depth of our darkness. He is the direction we look to in order to see God, and the direction we take to draw near to God. He embodies the UP arrow.

But not only UP, He turns us toward each other (SIDE) by teaching how to handle conflict, to forgive, to get rid of the anger and envy that sabotage friendships, and to make community impossible. He models the SIDE syllable and teaches us how to get along with each other.

And finally, DOWN. Jesus comes DOWN to our level, becoming human. He doesn't use the considerable advantages he has over us to lord anything over us. He uses his power to serve. He sacrifices himself for us. He understands his glory and majesty as a place of privilege from which to better the lives of those who cannot better their own lives. He comes DOWN to save us. This doesn't leave a bad taste in our mouths. We don't experience it as patronizing. It is empowering. It gives us relief, joy, and hope. Similarly, when we move DOWN in humble acts of service with the heart and hands of Jesus, we can expect to be experienced by others as we experience Jesus.

Note as well that because of the Holy Spirit's presence in us, we're not left marvelling at Jesus's example and striving to follow it. The Holy Spirit in us empowers us for each syllable. We move toward God as the Spirit in us propels us to intimacy with God. We don't strain to forgive; the Holy Spirit softens us inside and we gravitate naturally toward forgiveness. We don't grudgingly serve others; the Holy Spirit inside us gives us joy. The UPSIDEDOWN life is fuelled by the Holy Spirit.

Two sides then to anastatoo. The exegesis of UPSIDEDOWN and the love letter of UP SIDE DOWN. Turning the world UPSIDEDOWN as we turn UP to God, SIDE to each other, and DOWN in humble acts of service. The "what" and the "how" all tucked nicely into one package—a package we'll spend the rest of the book unpacking as we get more specific about the content of each syllable and look at some core beliefs and practices for each. But first, a little bit of clarity—in the form of a warning.

Hypocrite Is a One-syllable Word

Make sure you don't overemphasize one syllable. Christians (or churches, for that matter) tend to put an accent on one over the others. You need to be on your guard against being a monosyllabic Christian; each syllable is equally critical, and you need to fire on all syllables.

Shout out to all the mechanics at this point. I trust you are excited about this unexpected connection point with me. This author understands you. I'm more than just a white-collar pastor. I too have grease under my fingers and bloody knuckles. Granted, it's from working on my mountain bike and not my truck, but I feel it's enough to ensure mutual respect and legitimize my rephrasing of "firing on all cylinders" to "firing on all syllables." We're not that different, you and me. Although, I'm guessing I wear more spandex than you. Unless you wear spandex when you putter around the garage. I won't judge, but I am curious enough about your motivation to take a break from writing and google "mechanics in spandex." Not that long a break, as it turns out. I now return to writing with both an appreciation for safe search settings, and some slight nausea, that I did not have half a minute ago.

I once took my car to a rather absentminded mechanic and found out first-hand what it meant to not fire on all cylinders. It was frustrating. Not as frustrating as Cousin Aarons's experience with his absentminded proctologist, but still annoying, as a daydreaming mechanic can potentially turn an easy repair into a nightmare.

I had paid my $1,400 bill, picked up the keys, went to the parking lot, and started the vehicle. I expected to hear the smooth purring of a 2000 Lexus LX470. (May she rest in peace. Cause of death: a collision with a deer in the spring of 2020.) Instead of a purr, I heard a wheeze. Sexy Lexy started bucking like an asthmatic rodeo bull. It turns out the mechanic had crossed a few spark plug wires, and the result was a vehicle not firing on all cylinders. Kind of. I know technically this isn't exactly what was going on, but it's close enough. If there are any mechanics out there who feel like you need to send correction emails, I am willing to open them, but only if you attach a picture of yourself in spandex.

Let's make the connection: A 4.7-litre Lexus engine is designed to fire on eight cylinders, and when it doesn't, it sputters and shakes. It can hardly move. It's running on borrowed time. It feels like nothing is going to hold together for very long. Chaos is always around the corner. Of course, a human being isn't designed to run on eight cylinders, or any cylinders at all, for that matter! No, a human being is designed to fire on three syllables, and when it doesn't, it will sputter and shake, run on borrowed time, feel like it is about to fall apart, and chaos will always be around the corner.

This intellectually insulting analogy has the saving grace of being helpful. It immediately explains every concern you've had about Christians over the years. Every single one. "Not firing on all syllables" is the answer to all negative versions of the question "Why are some Christians so _____?" Those judgmental, greedy, or petty Christians? Whatever fits in the blank, the answer is the same: not firing on all syllables.

Too often we see this with elderly Christians. It's common to experience an older Christian sputtering along. You can tell they're not firing on all syllables because they cause chaos and pollute the atmosphere. Despite years of devoted church attendance, Grandpa causes carnage. He pits the kids against each other or distributes family resources unfairly or in ways that manipulate to his ends. Family gatherings, if they happen, inevitable end up with someone in tears. If not in the living room, then certainly on the way home as siblings or in-laws vent emotion about the toxic environment they've just been in. It ought to be a drive home celebrating the joy of being around someone who has been progressively transformed to be more and more like Jesus. Instead, it's spent licking wounds.

The person responsible for the pain gives the appearance of being devoutly religious. Perhaps it's a grandmother who prays for two hours a day and has led a Bible study in her home every Wednesday for the last twenty years. Maybe it's a tee-totalling uncle who has taught Sunday school forever, never once watched an R-rated movie, and who funded the placement of countless Bibles in bedside dressers in hotels. However, it is these religious people who are also breaking hearts and fracturing families with their poison. Why? They are usually firing on only one syllable. They accent on one and ignore the others.

Imagine a grandmother strong on the UP syllable. She would win a Bible trivia night. She's a prayer warrior. Her ability to discipline her thoughts is admirable. When praying, her mind doesn't wander to warm Brazilian nights with Fernando back in 1964. It isn't even hard for her to not think about his warm moonlight caresses, such is her devotion. She's exemplary in her UP-syllable strength. But her knowledge of scripture and prayer don't propel her toward acts of kindness and generosity. Instead, she uses her knowledge and devotion to position herself above others. Her considerable UP strength causes her to feel superior. She sees herself as more pious than those around her, fit to correct and judge them, and all in the name of promoting holiness. Her condemnation is reframed as discernment, her ignoring of the hurting as purity. This messed up way of thinking is common for those only firing on the UP syllable.

Transformation hasn't happened for this woman, at least to the extent that it should. If she had lived a truly UPSIDEDOWN life for fifty years, her grandkids would be flocking to her. Supper at her house would extend way into the evening because people wouldn't want to leave. The financial burdens of her descendants would be lessened by her deliberate and gracious generosity, and they would be grateful. Instead, visits are rare and grudging. Visitors watch the clock and are acutely aware of how much time they need to spend during the visit to not appear rude, but as soon as the magic moment arrives, everyone takes off. When she passes away, there will be some grief, but mainly her "loved ones" will feel guilt and relief. The years before she passes away, she will become increasingly bitter about how she's being treated. She understands people are avoiding her, but she doesn't know why. All she has ever done is try to follow Jesus as best she can. This unawareness is one of the true tragedies of a life not firing on all syllables.

It doesn't turn out any better for a SIDE-heavy Christian. He will risk co-dependency because he's not primarily sustained by his relationship with God (UP). He will need something from his community that community cannot provide. As he tries to take from others what he can only receive from God, he will suffocate them with his emotional neediness. Then, having drained everyone's emotional tank, he'll move on to a different group to suck dry. This continues for a few months, even years, as he cycles in and out of different churches or small groups. Eventually, he feels like he's not accepted. But that isn't true. People have accepted the reality of who he is. They have accepted he is the guy who sabotages community with his narcissistic neediness and are now avoiding him.

SIDE-syllable people have increasingly shrinking, little lives that end up dominating every group agenda, and people rightly tire of it. Without the purifying outlet of DOWN service and the worship of UP to keep their lives about something other than themselves, SIDE people stagnate and shrink. Having not hit all three syllables with consistency, they are ill-fit to turn the world UPSIDEDOWN. How could they? Turning the world UPSIDEDOWN requires people who themselves are being turned UP, SIDE, and DOWN. You can't give what you don't have.

When DOWN is emphasized, the problems are different but still crippling. DOWN Christians end up cynical. Helping others without the nourishing sustenance of UP and the supportive camaraderie of SIDE is impossible to sustain without becoming cynical. When those we are helping aren't receptive, improving, or even grateful, it's disheartening at best and infuriating at worst. Both the angry activist and the disillusioned pastor are victims of a heavy DOWN accent.

These scenarios are common but not inevitable, because you get to control what kind of Christian you become. Making sure you fire on all syllables ensures you don't become a monosyllabic tragedy. You can easily avoid the sort of fate I've been describing. Let's return to our first example of the bitter grandma to see how firing on all syllables might have saved her.

Toxic, praying Grandma would have ended up otherwise had she actively pursued the UPSIDEDOWN life instead of just UP. If she had insisted on forgiveness being as important as memorizing 1 Thessalonians. If she had forgiven Fernando for making promises with his hands that his heart didn't keep. Surely if she had elevated the importance of the SIDE syllable and lived in a community of confession, repentance, and forgiveness, the vulnerable accountability would have served to drain the toxins out of her system.

We see a similar detoxification effect as we imagine her engaging in the DOWN syllable. Imagine if she had committed to sacrificial generosity as part of following Jesus. Initially, she would have to discipline herself to do so, but eventually, generosity would become a gracious reflex. Imagine a lifetime of her working alongside hurting people instead of a lifetime judging them from a distance. Imagine if "those people" she judged from afar were instead people whose stories and names she knew. Her proximity to their pain would have kept her heart soft. It's safe to say that if she added SIDE and DOWN to her already rigorous UP practises, she wouldn't die lonely, because those who live the UPSIDEDOWN life don't die lonely—they die happy. The UPSIDEDOWN life is the best retirement plan available.

I suspect my example reminds you of a few in your life. We probably all have personal stories similar to this. But it's important to see that our lives don't just bear the pain of monosyllabic Christianity—history does. The brutal actions of Christians, both the petty, small, personal ones and the large-scale cataclysmic ones, are only possible when the accent is on one syllable. If you don't learn to fire on all syllables, you risk becoming an under-achieving Christian, the sort of person who causes pain. The sort of person who may think they are living for God's UPSIDEDOWN dream but is causing nightmares for others.

No one is perfect, and no one gets it right all the time. You may not ever fire perfectly on all syllables. *But just because no one gets it right all the time doesn't mean you allow yourself to get it wrong most of the time.* It's too simple a concept for you to have an excuse here. You need only hold all three syllables together as best you can. To avoid the tragedies of a monosyllabic life doesn't require perfection, but you do need to be intentional and committed. The UPSIDEDOWN life doesn't just happen.

Now, having scared the wits out of you—unless you don't mind the prospect of dying alone—let me move us in a cheerier direction. Firing on all syllables doesn't just happen, but that doesn't mean it's a burden. It is immensely helpful to have the UP, SIDE, and DOWN syllables guiding your life, as they help you make sense of what you might need to do in those times when you feel lost. Personally, the firing on all syllables concept has helped me on those days when I feel something is off.

You know those days when you feel on edge, lonely, or disoriented? Whatever it might be, something feels off. Often in those moments we move without thinking to that which offers comfort. We address what we're feeling with an ingrained reflex. Perhaps we head to the gym, the mall, the fridge, the computer, the arena, the walking path, or da club. Maybe we do something more obviously damaging, like succumb to an addiction or initiate a sexual encounter to distract or affirm. If you're a Christian, maybe you try to pray or read your Bible. Obviously, some of these behaviours are more harmful than others, but just because reading the Bible is less harmful than eating a tub of ice cream doesn't mean it's more helpful. Think of Grandma. Those things that look OK on the surface (reading your Bible) might actually be keeping you from doing what is best for you if they represent a repeated hitting of one syllable at the expense of the others. But now, because of the UPSIDEDOWN idea, you have a framework to use in those moments when you feel lostness or angst. The way forward is simply to ask: "Which syllable do I need to hit today?"

My tendency is to be an UP-syllable Christian. When I'm feeling off, I assume what I need is more prayer, learning, reading the Bible, or some other kind of UP syllable spiritual initiative. I can unthinkingly slide into that groove. But using the UPSIDEDOWN rubric, I realize I don't need to read another chapter of Thessalonians or write in my journal. UP isn't what's missing. It's just what I'm good at. It's where I find comfort, not necessarily what I need. I need to move in a SIDE or DOWN direction. I need to drop a gift card in someone's mailbox. I need to go for a walk with a friend. The UPSIDEDOWN rubric and the need to stay firing on all syllables helps me address what needs to be addressed and jars me out of my unthinking and blind pattens.

It will help you as well.

Maybe despite a rigorous schedule of prayer and Bible reading you still get irrationally angry when you're cut off in traffic. Probably more prayer isn't going to help. It hasn't so far! Maybe what you need is SIDE. A face-to-face confession of your sin. Or the healing power an authentic conversation about the struggles and joys in your life, about parenting, or finances, or stress, or areas of failure.

Maybe you've been volunteering, servicing, acting generously with your time and money and still feel like crap. You're angry at the world. Your DOWN syllable has been awesome, but the UP is basically shrivelled up. Take an afternoon to pray. Read the book of Mark. Go connect with God in the park. Hit that UP syllable a bit and start firing on all syllables.

Use the UP, SIDE, DOWN syllables as a diagnostic tool to understand what might be unbalanced as you follow Jesus. Of course, narrowing it down to which syllable you might need is only half the process. After diagnosing what's missing, there needs to be a prescription for how to find it. This is what we're going to do in Chapter 4, where we move from diagnosis to prescription. To do so will require turning my attention from engines (which I know little about) toward sailing (which I know even less about). I promise my limited knowledge will not stop me from trying to make it sound like I know what I'm talking about. I'd appreciate your help in this. My part is to sound like an expert. Your part is to assume that I am. It's mutually beneficial. This entire book will be a better read if you imagine me as an expert on anything I write about: cycling, sailing, parenting, cooking, New Testament scholarship, cigars, how to satisfy your partner, and the American Civil war. I could go on, but I don't want to spoil the excitement of the next chapters with an exhaustive list of my areas of expertise. Better for you to be dazzled in the moment than prepared ahead of time. Although there is one area I can claim no expertise in. Puzzles. Puzzles are for losers—take that, Cousin Aaron.

CHAPTER 4

The UPSIDEDOWN Sail

Jesus once had a late-night visitor. The visitor was curious about Jesus's teaching but couldn't afford to be seen fraternizing with a potential rebel rabbi like Jesus. The conversation we have recorded for us is short, but it includes a great line from Jesus:

"The wind blows where it wishes, and you hear its sound, but you don't know where it comes from or where it goes. So it is with everyone who is born of the Spirit." (John 3:8 English Standard Version)

Let's take Jesus up on his invitation to imagine the Holy Spirit as the wind and use that starting point to introduce another image: the UPSIDEDOWN sail.

Many of Jesus's friends were fishermen who fished on decent-sized inland lakes. We have records of storms on these lakes large enough to cause experienced fishermen and sailors to fear they might capsize and die. When Jesus mentions the Holy Spirit being like the wind, it's likely most of their imaginations would have gone to boats and water. We will go in the same direction because we are committed exegetes. Although as someone living on the landlocked prairies of Manitoba, Canada, I am about as familiar with sailing as I am with altitude sickness.

I can get the gist of what Jesus is saying because, as a cyclist on the bald Canadian prairies, I have learned the importance of paying attention to the wind. For too long I would take a quick look at the small flag on my neighbour's porch and see evidence of only a slight breeze. I'd head out the door and pedal into the countryside. Early in the ride, I'd feel I was having a great day. I'd be setting personal bests at every marker. I'd begin taking mental notes about what I'd eaten, and I'd commit it to memory so I could repeat this pattern in the hours before my next race. Soaring with energy, I'd make the confident decision to increase the length of my ride and continue past my planned turn around point.

My excitement would fade when I would flip the U-turn to head back home and immediately be faced with gale-force winds. Where did the hurricane came from? I swear there was no tailwind on the way out. I'm forty kilometres from home! Bucking this headwind means my return speed should average about 3.75 km/h. It's going to take me forever. I am out of water. I have no food. I have no hope. I will die out here.

You only get caught like this a few times before you learn to pay attention to even the slightest whisper of wind, because when you're cycling on the prairies, it always matters which way the wind is blowing. To fight against it intentionally is tiring and stupid. To get propelled along by it is exhilarating. I presume the same is true of sailing. The same is certainly true of life. We feel either tired or propelled, depending on our orientation to the direction the Spirit is moving. You only need to get caught a few times rowing against the wind of the Holy Spirit before you realize you never want to be in that predicament again. You know what happens when you stop living for the UPSIDEDOWN dream of God—you end up pushing against life; momentum dries up and fatigue sets in. You always want to have that wind at your back propelling you along. But how?

It's easy enough to catch the Holy Spirit wind. Notice that when Jesus says the "the Spirit blows wherever it pleases" he is not saying "the Spirit blows in a random direction." No, there are prevailing winds to catch, predictable gusts of the Spirit that are always moving in a direction that will bring about the overarching purposes of God. When we work to turn the world UPSIDEDOWN, like Paul and Silas did in their encounters with Lydia, the demon-possessed slave girl, and the jailer, we ensure that our rudder has the boat pointed in the right direction to have these winds always at our back. When we make the choice to aim our little vessel toward the UPSIDEDOWN dreams of God, we'll have the wind at our back. What is left, then, is to build the largest sail to catch as much of the Spirit wind as we can.

To get started building your sail, imagine the part of the sail that runs vertically up the mast as UP, the horizontal bottom as SIDE, and the angled part running downward from the top of the mast diagonally as DOWN. Apply this image to the stories of the previous chapter and we can see how the Christians who are heavy on one syllable at the exclusion of the others are sitting out in the boat and not moving anywhere. Why? Lives without sails don't move anywhere. You'll want to have each syllable keep pace with the others, since the limiting factor for sail size is your most neglected syllable. When all three syllables are not in sync, you end up with a ribbon, or a flag, on your boat, but not a sail.

To start building your sail, we will look at one core belief and two core behaviours per syllable. This means that by the end of the book, you will have three things to believe and six things to do, which will ensure your sail is able to catch the wind of the Spirit. It's about to get practical. Tamara will be proud.

UP

UP Core Belief: Jesus Is Lord

Not a controversial claim here. This phrase is all over the pages of the Bible and is still commonly used today without any real modification from its ancient use. If you haven't heard someone say it in church, or sing it in a song, you will soon. "Jesus is Lord" is what Christians believe and have always believed. It is central, essential, and thus, "core."

There are many common phrases Christians use that, because of the frequency in which they're used, are at risk for losing their meaning. An example of this is the phrase "in Jesus's name, Amen." This phrase ends most prayers and is most of the time mumbled out quickly with forks already poised to dig into the mashed potatoes, so the power of the phrase is missed. But it isn't missed by everyone. Every time someone says, "in Jesus's name," demons' and angels' ears perk up in fear and expectation of what might happen next, even when what happens next is the passing of the ketchup. We miss this. Similarly, "Jesus is Lord" is in danger of becoming the kind of thing you say without realizing that it's a potent phrase about identity and allegiance.

The first Christians got into a lot of hot water because they insisted "Jesus is Lord" instead of "Caesar is Lord." Since scalding was a common way of torturing those who opposed Caesar, the hot water they found themselves in was often literal. To call someone "Lord" was to say where your ultimate allegiance lay and who you believed had ultimate authority. This ultimate authority extended to dictating how you perceived reality. Since Caesar was Lord, when you had a difference of opinion with him, you gave way; you changed your mind, not him. And if you did disobey, you did it at your peril. The universe no longer backed you, since Caesar defined reality. This is what lords do.

You can see the threat and challenge "Jesus is Lord" presents. It's not what we might imagine to be a private religious claim. It wasn't a way to describe your personal spiritual belief. It wasn't a private opinion with no public ripple effects. The claim of Caesar and the Roman Empire was that "Caesar is Lord," and what they didn't mean was that he was someone to be privately worshipped in your own home; rather, he was the one running the show. This wasn't a situation in which your housemate down the hall lit a candle in her room and prayed to Caesar while you lit yours and prayed to Jesus and there was no tension because you could all have private individual spiritual values and then go out for lattes, because "to each their own." No. Jesus is Lord was, and remains, a universal claim with public implications.

Jesus is Lord (and not Caesar).

Jesus is Lord (and not the economy).

Jesus is Lord (and not the media).

Jesus is in control. He is the true king.

But we might also add something else in the brackets. This other addition emphasizes something closer to home.

Jesus is Lord (over me).

Or

Jesus is Lord (and I am not).

To say, "Jesus is Lord" is to offer your highest and most thorough allegiance. It's a statement that indicates you are giving up your personal freedom in order to pursue his dreams. But, as is always the case, the things we give up to follow Jesus turn out to be not much of a sacrifice compared to what we receive in return. In this case, consider how the core belief "Jesus is Lord" removes chaos from your life.

Think of how all the options you face regarding specific issues like forgiveness, marriage, and money now have focus. You now approach these as Jesus would have you approach them. Let's consider forgiveness first. Sure, there are those who are of the opinion that holding a grudge is a perfectly permissible thing to do, and it's also fine to seek revenge on the person who hurt you. They believe it's a dog-eat-dog world, and they have to look out for number one. But not you. You believe Jesus is Lord, so you take his convictions about reality as your own. Jesus doesn't believe in "every man for himself." Instead, he believes in a world where forgiveness is power, God is protecting you, and revenge is sinful. Your core belief is Jesus's version of reality (Jesus is Lord), so you will obey him. Your microdecision to forgive and not seek revenge is easily made because it flows out of the big decision that if you and Jesus have a difference of opinion about something, you will go with him. He is Lord.

Your thinking flows along these lines:

> *I am mad and hurt. Jesus says I am to forgive those who hurt me. I don't want to. It doesn't feel like it makes sense. That doesn't matter. Jesus knows things about how reality works that I don't. Jesus is Lord (and I am not). I will forgive.*

Or perhaps you believe that "living together" before getting married is a wise move. It lets a couple get to know each other better without the risks, and potential complexity, of a marriage breaking down at a later point. Except Jesus believes love needs to grow in the protected environment of long-term commitment, and sexual relationships are deeply spiritual; they teach you something sacred about God. He doesn't desire for you to be a part of any sort of trial, or "try-out," relationship that might needlessly damage you or cheapen how you see God. Since you believe that Jesus is right and you should obey him, the path you walk through sexual relationships and toward marriage is abundantly clear. There is a bunch of thinking you don't need to do once you've settled on doing it Jesus's way.

Jesus is Lord. He is right. And when I have a different opinion, I am wrong. I can't say, "No, Lord" with a straight face, because he ceases to be Lord when I do that. This one simple foundational belief guides you in forming other beliefs until, eventually, you have what the Bible terms "the mind of Christ"—thinking like him instead of believing the right things about him.

Initially, you might feel like his opinions are imposed on reality, like you're having to do things that don't make sense and are harder than your old life. But then you feel a strong gust of Spirit wind propelling you along with momentum and joy, and you realize you are now aligned with reality and your sail is that much bigger. You were wrong, and Jesus was right. Jesus is always right. This is because he has no opinions; he only describes reality. You'll realize this soon enough as your obedience to him aligns you with reality and you feel the wind at your back. It all starts with the core belief: Jesus is Lord. Now, let's turn our attention to the two core UP practices.

UP Core Practice #1: Daily Devotions

When I was in high school, my parents lived in a three-storey century home. My bedroom was the entire third floor attic, which meant coming down to the kitchen for breakfast involved a descent of four flights of stairs. The location of the last flight of stairs meant that most mornings I would see my dad's feet as he sat on the couch reading his Bible, praying, and journaling. Monday to Friday, with very few exceptions, Dad would get up and have his devotions from 6 a.m.–7 a.m. His signal when the hour was up seemed to be hearing me coming down for breakfast. He'd tuck his Bible and notebook under the couch and move on to the next part of his day.

Every now and then, I'd sneak his journal out from under the couch and read a bit of it. I'd read the prayer requests he wrote out and see what he was praying for regarding me or my sisters. I'd see the names of people at work he was trying to muster up the courage to invite to church. I suspect he knew I was reading it, because anytime something got a little more interesting, the penmanship would get indecipherable. You don't want your kids reading your personal confessions to Jesus. He was wise to make certain parts unreadable.

I now do what he did. I have my 6 a.m.–7 a.m. devotional routine. I also suspect my kids of spying on me so have to turn my writing into an illegible scrawl as necessary. Although I do try to have a little more fun with them than my dad did with me. To mess with them, I'll write something like "murder," "smuggle," or "dispose of" and then make sure the next words I write are impossible to make out. Occasionally, I'll write a prayer in which I celebrate the joys of conjugal bliss, with a poetic vividness that would make Pablo Neruda blush.

Security measures notwithstanding, this daily devotional practice, the one my dad cultivated and whose pattern I inherited, is the first core practice of the UP syllable. It is through this daily practice that you get to know Jesus better. This time spent talking with Jesus is essential; intuitively we know this is important. How do we learn to trust unless we spend the time it takes to build trust? How do we fall in love unless we spend time? How do you learn to follow someone, to mimic their behavioural patterns and thinking, unless you're in close enough proximity to observe them? We want Jesus's characteristics to rub off on us, and they can't if we aren't getting close enough to him. It's easy to see why the daily pattern of focusing your attention intently on Jesus through prayer and reading the Bible is essential.

Most new Christians get this. They intuitively understand the theoretical importance of a daily devotional practice and are often eager to develop the habits and patterns that lead them to knowing Jesus better. But their momentum is interrupted by two things. Let's take a look at them so that you, as a new Christian, can be prepared for them when they come.

First, they realize devotions are surprisingly hard. The new Christian sets her alarm for 5:45 a.m. She stumbles out of bed, makes a cup of coffee, and lights a candle. She pulls out a blank journal and clicks her pen a few times. After adjusting the cushions on the couch, she puts her feet up and flips open the journal and her Bible. She is ready to be bathed in holy light, but then nothing happens. That is not entirely true—frustration is happening. She's frustrated as she reads and then re-reads the opening parts of Genesis. She's starting at the beginning, since it only makes sense that you would start there. Except it has nothing to do with Jesus, it contradicts everything she has been taught about human origins, and it involves talking snakes. It talks about one man naming every animal. If she manages to hang on until Genesis 6, she'll be treated to stories of otherworldly beings mating with human women. She won't be too sure what to journal about that part.

OK, she says. Not so sure about the Bible reading part. Let's try praying. She begins to pray silently, thinking thoughts and assuming Jesus can hear them. About twenty seconds later, her mind is wandering. She decides to try praying out loud. This helps her stay focused, but it seems more like she's trying to impress an imaginary audience with her amazing words. It feels inauthentic, so she goes back to praying in her head, but her mind wanders to Joel Osteen. She hasn't been a Christian for that long, but she knows enough to know it's not a great prayer session when it involves imagining a shirtless Joel frolicking in the surf.

Having failed at Bible reading and prayer, she turns to journaling. She writes the date at the top of the page. She pauses and then writes the time at the top of the page. It might turn out to be important that it was 6:05 a.m. Has it really only been five minutes? She looks at the window and then writes, "Sunny day today" as her first line. She's not sure exactly how it happened, but the next thing she remembers is waking up with her ear wet from the little pool of drool accumulating between her slumped head and the carefully arranged cushion. She wakes up with a sore neck and a guilty conscience. It was like her and Jesus's first date, and she fell asleep. He must be so bored with her. Although wasn't he the problem? She showed up, lit the candles, and read the Bible. She tried to make this work, but Jesus didn't do anything!

It turns out having devotions is harder than she thought. She thought it was going to be as exciting as binge-watching Netflix, but it was more like trying to stay awake while someone explains Rubik's Cube algorithms to you.

Realizing there must be something she's missing, she seeks out a more experienced Christian and asks for help. This reaching out is a wise idea in theory, but unfortunately it can lead to the second experience that slows devotional momentum. If the person being reached out to as a mentor doesn't have much of a devotional life herself, the situation backfires. The new Christian has approached someone to help her learn how to succeed with an essential practice and comes away feeling like prayer and reading the Bible are optional.

I was naively surprised to learn that my dad's pattern of prayer and scripture reading was not the norm. My friends, most of whom had Christian dads, would see my dad's journal lying around and would ask questions about the presence of this devotional "props." I realized many of their dads didn't do what my dad did. I was surprised, because they were regulars at church, and it's not like their dads were ashamed to identify as followers of Jesus. Like a new believer approaching a potential mentor only to be surprised by the lack of example, I was surprised when I realized some people thought of themselves as followers of Jesus yet didn't pray and read their Bible in a disciplined, intentional way.

Surprise should be an appropriate reaction when you find a Christian who doesn't daily set aside a time to pray and read his Bible. We should be surprised—they are core practices, after all. They shape you profoundly. True, reading your Bible and praying from 6 a.m.–7 a.m. doesn't guarantee Christian maturity. I'm sure you can find a miserable Christian who does daily devotions. The potential exists for someone to have such lopsidedly emphasized on the UP syllable that her relationships are a mess and her service to others is nil. You can still be a miserable SOB and read your Bible and pray every day.

However, it's crucial to understand that while you might find a miserable Christian who does devotions, you won't be able to find a strong Christian who doesn't. This is why the practice is core. You have to do it if you want to follow Jesus well. You can't follow Jesus without reading the Bible and praying, not only because that's what Jesus wants, but because that's what Jesus DID. He prayed and studied the Bible with tenacity, discipline, and passion. Mimicking his devotional practices are non-negotiable for those who claim to follow him.

I'm stating it strongly because it needs to be stated strongly. When we make optional what needs to be a central priority, we suffer, and many followers of Jesus are suffering as they miss out on what they could become if they prioritized the UP core practices. Their neglect of these practices might be because no one insisted on them. No one bothered to tell them to wipe the drool from their cheek and try again, and again, and again until those early morning moments with Jesus shifted from being a frustrating or embarrassing experience to being the most cherished and precious parts of their entire life. Because that is what will happen. But you need to be prepared to learn some new skills and develop a bit of discipline. Make yourself do it for a while. I'm talking a few solid months. Be patient with yourself as you get better at concentrating. It takes practise to learn to listen to Jesus. Don't worry if you don't understand everything you read. When you find something you don't get, ask Jesus questions about it. Write down any fool thought that comes into your head and don't despise any of these awkward and frustrating first steps; Jesus sure doesn't! When you take your wobbly first steps toward Jesus, he can't keep the grin off his face. His arms are open in front of you in welcome. He is delighted you showed up! His delight is important to note. It will sustain you when devotions feel like they're doing nothing for you, because you'll be reminded that your devotions are doing something for him.

One of the most helpful perspectives you can have—one which will help you push on until your devotional time begins to deliver some of what you hoped it will—is this: see your devotional time as giving Jesus attention and honour. See it as a time that means something to him. That no matter how much or little you "get" out of it, he is receiving something precious from you. This allows you to be indifferent toward the results, to not worry that you're doing something wrong because you aren't getting the devotional buzz you anticipated. Even if nothing is happening for you, something is happening for him.

In fact, it's often in this place, where you are entirely indifferent about what you're feeling, that you will begin to feel something. You laying aside your agenda, which is what I mean by "indifference," allows him to direct your attention to what he wants you to see and experience. If you present Jesus with a script, he doesn't generally read it. Nor should he. He knows what we deeply need and will give it to us in the way we need it at the time we need it. Come with a blank slate.

Practically, a sample devotion time, for those of you who are curious, looks something like this.

Start by giving thanks to Jesus for a few things. Tell him you are excited about spending time with him and learning about him. Tell him you're excited to receive whatever he has for you. Then read a chapter of Psalms. Read it slowly. Think about how the emotions expressed in the psalm might relate to your life. Write a few thoughts down. Then read a chapter from Matthew, Mark, Luke, or John. Imagine being in the scene with Jesus. Which character do you relate to? How would you feel if you were there? How does that inform your life today? Write a few more thoughts down and then ask the Holy Spirit to help you love the people around you today like Jesus would if he were you. If anything specific comes to mind, pray about that.

This whole process probably takes about twenty-five minutes, and it's a great start. It should be a goal as you get better at this to extend your time to an hour. You will get better at it—every aspect of it. So good that eventually the hour will pass quickly and you'll no longer be disciplining yourself to do this. You will be anticipating it. Eventually, you notice a pattern. The days in your life when you feel most alive, most like yourself, are the days when you spent a good chunk of time in the morning with Jesus. The tough days, the days when you stepped out of line or hurt someone, are usually the days you skipped devotions. That realization alone will have you eager to maintain and grow the pattern of daily devotions. It will become fuel for the rest of your life.

UP Core Practice #2: Witnessing

The second UP core practice is witnessing. Witnessing is telling others about Jesus. You already know witnessing is critical. You only have to think of your own story. Who invited you to take your first steps toward Jesus? Maybe someone invited you to church with them. Maybe when you were talking with a friend about a breakup they sheepishly said something like,

"The only thing I know that might help is Jesus. Can I tell you about him?" At that stage you would have listened to someone talk about the power of unicorns if it meant you might be able to put the pieces of your heart back together, so you gave them the green light.

Maybe you couldn't shake either the hunger for something more or the hunch that there was something more. So when a friend invited you to church, you said, "Hell, yes!" Because you had quite a mouth on you back then. Maybe you weren't feeling any real level of discontent. You just got invited to help a friend with her church's inner city literacy project and wanted to make a difference. Your involvement in sharing the love of Jesus by teaching kids how to read ended up being the first step toward Jesus. You found yourself enjoying the company of those who followed him, you were mesmerized by the prayer time beforehand, and eventually you just asked, "So can just anybody come to your church on a Sunday morning?" And the friend who invited you to help with the project broke into a big grin. You realized she was hoping for this right from the beginning.

That person who nudged you closer to Jesus, however big or small that nudge was, was witnessing—and now you get to be a witness as well, because it's one of the UP core practices. Jesus intends for us to point people UP toward him. We know this is true because he tells his first little band of followers "you will be my witnesses," and we have no reason to think he has changed his mind about what he wants his followers to do.

The word "witness" is a multifaceted word, and it's important to understand what Jesus meant by it. To be a witness is to tell the story of what you have seen or experienced. I've probably already squeezed every drop I could out of courtroom analogies when I imagined Paul and Silas on trial, but here I go again anyway. We're familiar with witnesses in a legal setting. "The prosecution would like to call its next witness, Your Honour." And the jury looks on with sympathy as the little old lady hobbles to the impossibly high step leading to the witness stand to share the agony she experienced at the hands of a corrupt multinational corporation and its legion of high-priced lawyers. Her testimony as a witness is going to set the record straight.

This overall image is helpful as we start articulating what distinctly Christian witness means, provided your mental image of the courtroom doesn't include backroom deals with the judge, bribing of juries, and getting romantically involved with your client. The "flirt-to-convert" strategy is a bad witnessing plan. But the little old lady on the stand isn't flirty, just honest. What she's going to do as a witness is tell the story of what she has seen and heard. She promises to tell the entire truth and nothing but the truth and knows God will help her. The jury will be convinced by her testimony, provided it connects with reality as they understand it and with their values and priorities.

Her testimony will need to be tapered to land well with the jury. A wise lawyer will know this and guide the little old lady to emphasize a certain part of her testimony over another based on the composition of the jury. She should probably downplay the part about her beach house in Malibu if the jury is made up of laid-off factory workers. She's wise to do this so they can hear the important parts of her story and not get hung up on what is not central. The multinational corporation is corrupt whether the little old lady resides in a palatial beach house or an underpowered 1984 minivan. But still, it's wise to make sure you aren't sharing your testimony in a way that includes needless and unhelpful distractions. In the same way, each of us needs to be aware of who it is we're witnessing to so we can share the parts of our life with Jesus that will most resonate with them.

What you say to the agnostic physician is going to be different than how you witness to a practising psychic. Perhaps the physician will be curious to hear how an addiction you battled for decades is no longer a problem after three months of having devotions. Or perhaps they'd be interested to hear you ask if they would be supportive of you weaning yourself off a sleeping pill prescription. You sleep much more peacefully since you started following Jesus and suspect you might be able to sleep OK now. Now please, don't stop taking any prescription medicine because of this paragraph. This is only an example of the kind of thing that can happen for followers of Jesus that might be of interest to a physician. And, of course, part of being a wise witness to a physician is to not appear like a religious quack who immediately takes herself off prescribed medicine. But a measured and strategic conversation about the new strength you're finding as you follow Jesus is potentially a powerful witness.

For the psychic, your witness is going to be different. Maybe you have first-hand experience of praying for someone and as you were praying it became clear he was being oppressed by an evil spirit. You prayed for this evil spirit to leave "in Jesus's name" and were amazed at how powerful his name is in the spiritual realm, because the evil spirit left. You ask your psychic friend what they do when things get scary during a séance, or when he's communicating with spirits. Whose name does he invoke to get results?

I once had this exact conversation with a couple of Indigenous spiritual leaders. I was surprised to hear that when they're discerning spirits in their ceremonies or want to protect someone being attacked by an evil spirit, they won't hesitate to use the name of Jesus. It led to a remarkable conversation about the majesty and glory of Jesus and his role in the unseen realm.

Witnessing shouldn't be intimidating. With a little wisdom and a little courage, you'll find plenty of opportunities to share your faith. Often when you begin to share your story, you find that Jesus has already been at work in the life of the person you're talking with, preparing her to receive what you have to share. Jesus is committed to drawing all people to himself and is actively pursuing them in ways we can't see or even imagine. This means that part of witnessing is listening to where Jesus is already at work in someone's life and helping her discover that.

Important to note: witnessing doesn't always involve speaking. Often the most convincing witnesses do their convincing with actions and not words. Talk can be cheap, but people notice when someone is loving, joyous, peaceful, patient, and kind, because most people aren't. But as a follower of Jesus who is filled by the Spirit, you are! You can see the link here between daily devotions and strength of witness. Without the daily morning fuel up of Jesus's love, joy, and peace, you aren't able to have it flow out of you. The best witnessing strategy is to become so magnetic with love that people are drawn to you, and then you point them to Jesus. This means, at a really bare bones level, that you have to be likeable to be an effective witness. One of my regrets is that for about half my life, I missed the obvious—that likability was essential.

When I was in my early twenties, I was planning on starting a church. When I dreamed about who would be attending this church, I imagined people my age. Specifically on my heart was a group of fellow university students I was working with at a summer camp for mentally challenged adults. There were about twelve of us. A nice number to start a church with.

Later in the summer, I was driving with a friend of mine who knew all these people. I was sharing with him my dream to see them all come to this new church and get to know Jesus. His response?

"They won't go to your church."

"Why?"

"None of them like you."

"What does that have to do with it?"

I don't remember if I said that last line out loud, but I sure thought it. What did their liking me have to do with the truth of Jesus's majesty, teachings, resurrection, and plan for their lives?

Everything.

The truth of Christian witnesses is that they will love you before they love Jesus, which is OK. Jesus's plan is to make you lovable. This is good news for those who don't know what to say. You don't have to know what to say, because your life will speak. In the same way, if your life is speaking the wrong thing, it won't matter how convincing your arguments are.

So witnessing doesn't require a degree in theology or a massive vocabulary, but it will require you to be intentional. A great way to remain intentional is to make witnessing a part of your daily devotional practice. Set up shop in Starbucks with the biggest hardcover Bible you can find and pray out loud. I'm joking. Rather, during your devotional time, list in your journal the names of the people you wish were following Jesus. Pray for them every day, for them to be curious about and hungry for God. Pray that they will like you and for your relationship with them to grow. Praying prayers like these not only help you be intentional, but they have the effect of growing your compassion and interest in the people you're praying for. You'll need to have your affection for them grow so that you can stay motivated to witness. Many of the people we witness to take a long time to come to Jesus.

For the last fifteen years, I've been praying for twenty friends to make decisions to follow Christ. You'd see their names in my journal, not every day, but regularly. So far, four of the twenty have decided to follow Jesus. Not staggering results, but not bad considering how few adults tend to make this decision. You four know who you are, and this book is for you. At least for now. When the other sixteen decide to follow Jesus, I'll give them a signed copy as well. The signature will be all blurry from my happy tears, if my tear ducts still work by then. The remaining sixteen friends are taking their sweet time.

I can take some solace in the fact that the sixteen all really like me. I'm different than I was when I was thinking about starting a church and my buddy told me no one would come. These guys don't go to church, but if they did, they'd come to mine. God has changed me and made me more like Jesus. God isn't finished with me yet, and he also isn't finished with them.

SIDE

SIDE Core Belief: You Can't Follow Jesus And Not Prioritize Your Involvement In A Local Church

I imagine there will be strong pushback about the SIDE core belief.

Pushback from the stoners.

"Dude. I don't know about this core belief. You see, I love Jesus but not the church. It's kinda more like a private thing I got going on with him."

Pushback from the soccer moms.

"Pastor Nathan, I can appreciate what you're trying to say here, but it isn't helpful to say it as if it's black and white. Words like 'can't' and 'not' and 'local' are so rigid. Wisdom would suggest making your point a little less aggressively."

Pushback from my editor.

"You stopped trying to be funny fifteen pages ago and now you're picking it up again? Too scattered and inconsistent."

I'm no idiot. When both stoners and soccer moms express serious misgivings about an idea, maybe you should rethink it. Especially since if I lose soccer moms and stoners, I lose two of my three targeted demographics and I am left marketing this book exclusively to potato farmers. Wisdom directs me to listen, so I will rephrase what I wrote earlier. Here is my second crack at the core SIDE belief:

Unless you are prioritizing church, you are pretending to follow Jesus.

"Duuuuuuude! No man, that is not better at all!"

The soccer mom has not directly responded, but I notice she updated her FB status with a passive-aggressive:

"Looking forward to spending some much-needed time me time this Sunday! #happywifehappylife."

I don't mind this sort of pushback. It's exactly what should be anticipated when you elevate the importance of something higher than people are comfortable with. Like daily devotions, many followers of Jesus see prioritizing involvement in a local church as optional, so there's pushback when it's suggested otherwise.

It's worth asking how they got to the place where church involvement slid into the optional column, because even a casual glance at the New Testament (NT) shows it's anything but optional. I won't bother to make a list here of Bible verses that affirm my position. And it isn't just verses. Every NT book takes the idea that local church involvement is part of following Jesus. You'll see it for yourself, so I'll basically leave you on your own as you read through the Bible in your daily devotions. You'll quickly find evidence that Jesus would rather have you frequently meet with other Christians than do your laundry or have "me time." Indeed, you will have to ignore a lot of evidence to arrive at the conclusion that church is not a priority.

The love-letter approach won't save you here, either. It isn't an option to do a little shuffle that goes, "Yeah, sure, if you use a technical exegetical approach it's clear the authors want us in church, but Jesus has sent me a private message telling it isn't that big a deal." Hard to imagine this ever happening. Jesus died for the church. It's his first love. He isn't going to tell you it fits in the optional column. He didn't see it that way. It fits in the "to die for" column.

Even if the evidence in the Bible wasn't so consistent and obvious, you could still make a case for prioritizing involvement in a local church based on basic logic. Ask yourself how likely you are to turn the world UPSIDEDOWN on your own. The entire dream of God, the mission of those who follow Jesus, is of a magnitude to require a certain level of teamwork and community. Do I actually think I'm going to do that by myself?

It's only when you see the mission as being something personal for you, instead of the transformation of the whole world, that you could ever think following Jesus was a solo journey. I suppose if you thought the reasons Jesus wants us to follow him are a) so you can have powerful private spiritual experiences with him, or b) so you can get to heaven when you die, then you might be excused for assuming you don't need to prioritize church. Except those aren't the reasons Jesus wants you to follow him. He wants you to follow him so you can help turn the world UPSIDEDOWN. When you bail on the UPSIDEDOWN dream, trading it for a narrow, personal spirituality, you are no longer following Jesus, because you wandered off the path he is leading you down.

Don't mistake the few times when, in a roundabout way, he talked about the afterlife as that being the core of his message. You'll need to do exegesis on those passages to save you from projecting meaning onto them which Jesus didn't intend. And don't allow your own therapeutic, narcissistic culture to convince you that Jesus's priority is to make sure you're doing OK. Of course he is going to take care of his followers forever, and of course following him is going to bring joy. But those are by-products of following him; they are not his goal. We know what he's aiming for. Jesus wants, and wants his followers, to turn the world UPSIDEDOWN. And for that, you need the help of a church.

SIDE Core Practice #1: Prioritize Church Attendance

Out of this core belief comes the first predictable core practice: prioritize church attendance. Prioritize going to church over everything else. Prioritize your small group over everything else. If you're serious about following Jesus, you'll find that he leads you right smack into the middle of a church. The depth of your relationship with Jesus will slow down every time you miss a Sunday or any other day. This is simply true.

What this means is that you may have to endure a bit of low-level persecution. When you act as if Jesus thinks it's more important for you to serve and attend at your church than to be at every one of your kids' Sunday sports tournaments, or to go camping, people will push back. When you choose to prioritize church over other things, people will think you're odd. Sadly, you can anticipate at least some of this pushback coming from other Christians.

Now, lest you imagine this prioritization of church will mean endless drudgery à la, "You mean I can't play Ultimate Frisbee anymore at 9 a.m. on Sunday? BUT I LOVE FRISBEE . . . I LOVE FRISBEE" or "But then my daughter might not be able to make the Tier 15 regional softball all stars, because tryouts and games are all Sunday morning," let me soften what seems to be a hard line. Two ways to soften it.

First, I skip a few Sundays a year for mountain-bike racing. We're talking about seven to nine Sundays. I'm about 39/52 at our weekly small group. And finally, the weekly accountability group I have with two other guys usually ends up being monthly over the summer and bi-weekly the rest of the year. So I'm not nailing this 100 per cent myself, and I'm not asking you for perfection either. But—and this is the part I really want you to get—when I skip these things, I do acknowledge that I'm taking a step backwards. It would be wrong for me to pretend otherwise.

I could argue that flying down some flowing single track with the wind in my face is as worshipful an experience as church, but I'd be wrong. Since my dominant syllable is UP, that part of my sail is in pretty good shape. More than another solo experience of Jesus, I need to lengthen the SIDE part of my sail and church community does this. When I skip, my sail isn't as large as it could be. My skipping church is never neutral; it is harmful. Now having said that, I'm OK with you missing as much as me; to push you to do more than I'm doing would be hypocritical. I give you a free pass until you get into double-digit absenteeism. You're welcome.

The second way to soften my rigorous insistence on attendance is to talk about what you can expect when you do prioritize church participation. You'll enjoy the encouragement that comes as you grow. As you invest time in the rhythms and habits that actually grow a person, like church attendance, you'll be encouraged at the pace of your personal transformation. People who attend church, or church things, once a month grow at a once-a-month pace. This principle makes sense. No one is shocked that people who run once a month run marathons at a once-a-month pace, which is to say exceedingly slowly. When you prioritize attendance, you'll be encouraged how fast you grow.

You could even make the case that coming to church periodically is more discouraging than not coming at all. If you've ever lifted weights irregularly, you know how painful it is—especially squats. I was one of those who didn't so much skip leg day in the gym—I didn't schedule a leg day ever. But then I would read some muscle magazine and realize that unless you work out your legs, you're going to have terrible tragedy befall you, so I'd head to the gym and do a bunch of squats. Two days later I could hardly move. I'd howl like a wolf being poked with a sharp stick when I sat down on the toilet. I'd kind of have to roll my way off the toilet seat. It made for much awkwardness in public bathrooms. Except for that one time where it helped me make a new friend.

I'm comfortable saying that my intermittent attempts at squatting were harder on me than never squatting at all. It would take me forever to recover. I was also stuck in a place where I kind of knew it was important to do squats, but they weren't enough of a priority to focus on. This put me in the unenviable position of still caring, and because I cared, I was humiliated to be so far behind the people who squatted regularly. I felt people were probably judging me as they were imagining (rightly) pencil-thin legs under my sweats.

People who intermittently attend church commonly complain about feeling judged. It's the same kind of thing as my squat example. They still care enough to value what church offers, but they aren't committed enough to pursue it. This lukewarm state is the most difficult place to be emotionally. Isolated from community, they get paranoid and project things on people that aren't there. They assume people are judging them, but really, they're judging themselves for not pursuing what they know they should. But since they're not in a church community that could help them figure this out, they drift farther away from the "judgy" people at church. If they got to actually know people, and this would require involvement, they would find that they're not being judged at all. Instead, they would discover that people are rooting for them.

Consistent church attendance will help you feel supported. Your participation will result in your spiritual growth, and people will see that. You'll have people around you to affirm that growth. That affirmation from others is critical for those times when you feel like no progress is being made. It's notoriously hard to gauge your progress in becoming like Jesus without people around to comment on it and affirm it.

A couple of years ago, we had the privilege to welcome two young men into our family. I mentioned Truffles earlier, but I haven't mentioned his brother "Clicky." Truffles and Clicky were eleven and fifteen when they came to live with us. The neighbourhood they were from was occasionally dangerous, so they weren't used to playing outside. It wasn't their fault, but it meant they spent a lot of time inside on the couch. That changed when they came to our house. We do a lot of outdoor activities, and both boys gradually got in better shape as they adjusted to their new reality.

Now, I write this as someone who has been out of shape himself. I remember early in our marriage going for a hike in North Vancouver with Tamara at a place called the Grouse Grind. The hike starts in the parking lot and as soon as you exit, you start climbing stairs up the side of Grouse Mountain. You do this for a couple of hours without reprieve. I was determined to show Tamara what a specimen she'd married, so I whipped off my shirt and took off at a blistering pace, fully aware of how my torso was glistening sexily in the morning sun.

We hadn't done a hike like this before, and I played the situation all wrong. Sure, she was, and remains, a sucker for my naked torso, but what I didn't know was that she was in much better shape than I was. I was wrongly anticipating that she would begin to lag behind and then I could shift to a more comfortable and sustainable pace personally and never let her know that I was basically deep in the hurt locker as soon as we left the parking lot. She never faded. Five minutes in I downgraded my intentions from "impressing her" to "keeping up with her" as she pulled ahead.

I did manage to keep up with her for some time, a brief amount of time, possibly another three or four more minutes. I stared at her bum to motivate myself. This distraction bought me another two minutes. At least I think it was two minutes. I checked my watch to see how much time had gone by and was surprised to see two watches. Double vision is a bad sign. Although seeing two bums was not all bad. I slowed down. I offered excuses.

It must have been something we had a breakfast. She reminded me that I had a banana and granola, so probably not that. I then blamed the sandwich I had for lunch the day before when she wasn't around. She looked skeptical, but we'd only been married for a month and were in a stage of marriage where you'd prefer your spouse not look like an out of shape buffoon, so she let it go. In as casual a tone as I could manage, I told her to go on ahead and I'd catch up as soon as I felt better.

I never did feel better. A group of little old ladies passed me. A guy giving a piggyback to his kid passed me. A little old lady giving a piggyback to another little old lady passed me. I didn't catch Tamara, although we did cross paths again on the hike when she started back down the path after waiting for me at the top. She had waited so long she'd begun to worry that something had happened to me. Was I unconscious? Was I dead? She cried tears of relief, which I found tremendously embarrassing. My consolations for her driving home my own shame: "There, there, honey, it's OK. I didn't die. I just am really out of shape." Please keep this self-deprecating story in mind as I tell the story of one of our first hikes with one of our foster sons to remind yourself that I'm writing with an empathetic tone. I know what it feels like to be out of gas and embarrassed about it.

Eleven-year-old Truffles had already dropped nearly twenty pounds in the eight months he'd been in our house. He'd been riding his bike and playing road hockey and was in the best shape of his young life. But still not quite at the place where an eleven-kilometre hike to the top of mountainside cliffs is an easy expedition. But the day was clear, and the view would be spectacular, so off we went to the Enderby Cliffs, just outside Vernon, British Columbia, where we were holidaying.

About a mile in, Truffles was not a happy camper. The grade wasn't quite Grouse Grind steep, but it was still closer to climbing stairs than it was to walking down a hallway. Truffles started to fall off the pace. He began to feel powerful emotions. He pretty much walked through the whole Kübler-Ross grief progression. Denial—I can't believe we're doing this. Anger—I'm gonna throw myself off the top and that will teach you guys for hauling me up here. Sadness—I miss flat land. Resignation—Oh well, it is what it is. Actually there was no progression. He stayed mainly on anger.

I tried every trick in my repertoire to get him moving and motivated. I'd coached kids' mountain biking and hockey for years and had a lot of tools in my adolescent motivation toolbox. I can usually get even the most apathetic kid excited. Truffles was not buying any of it. Adding to the difficulty of motivating him was the series of crushing disappointments as each peak we crested turned out to only reveal three of four more further ahead. The actual top was not in view. This meant some of my motivation tactics were backfiring. When you're saying things like, "We're almost at the top! Can you see it? When we get there, we'll have our lunch!" but it turns out you're nowhere near the turnaround point, it's understandably demoralizing.

I knew I needed to change my angle of approach, so I did. Instead of pointing at the top, which seemed to always be moving farther away, I started to emphasize how far we'd come.

"Truffles, what's the longest distance you've ever walked before?"

"I dunno. Maybe to my friend's house."

"How far was that?"

"About four houses down from the school." (This is about four hundred metres.)

"Wow, that means even if we stopped right now, you would have already walked farther than you've ever walked in your whole life!"

"Hmm."

There was hope in that "Hmm," and I began to lay it on thicker.

"And plus, this is twice as hard as a normal walk, because most of it is almost straight up."

"Hmmmmm." (I added some "ms" so you can sense the mmmmmoood shifting.)

"Who in your class do you think could walk five kilometres straight up a hill in only half an hour?"

"Probably no one."

"It just might be that you've walked farther and faster up this hill than any other kid from Manitoba has ever walked up this hill."

And then the masterstroke parenting move.

"Hey, stop for a second and look back. Can you see through the trees? Way over there? See that grey speck? There's Sexy Lexy (before colliding with deer) in the parking lot! Look how far you have come!"

It didn't happen immediately, but slowly his pace quickened. I caught him sneaking glances back at the vehicle. Eventually, his mood changed, and it was sunshine and roses for him the rest of the way. He just needed to see how far he'd already come, and you do too.

You need to know how far you've come so that you can be encouraged that you're farther along the path with Jesus than you might know. Yes, there are lofty mountain peaks off in the distance where the saints are marching along at a higher altitude than you, and that might make you feel overwhelmed and doubtful you'll ever get there. This doubt can make your pace slow a bit. You might even turn around and give up.

You don't need a church community around you to show you these peaks. Reading your Bible or Christian biographies will establish for you pretty quickly that you're nowhere near your destination. Miles and miles to go before you totally become like Jesus, and, in fact, the journey never ends. But you will need a church community around you to show you how far you've come. To see accurately how far you've come requires having other people know you well. People who can stand with you in your moments when the peaks seem impossibly far off and can remind you of where you used to be and how far you've come. This happens when you prioritize church attendance and participation.

SIDE Core Practice #2: Forgive Those Who Disappoint You

It's a central conviction of the Christian faith that we are to forgive everyone who wrongs us. This is crystal clear. There are clear statements in the Bible to "forgive as the Lord forgave you" (Col 3:13 NIV). Instructions for prayer including lines like "forgive us our sins as we have forgiven those who sin against us" and "if you refuse to forgive others, your Father will not forgive your sins" (Mt 6:12,15 NLT). Forgiveness is a big deal for those who follow Jesus. He wants us to forgive others for absolutely everything.

Given that we're told to forgive every single wrong committed against us, why would I narrow the core practice to forgiving disappointment? Thanks for asking. I love an engaged and inquisitive reader. Especially ones like you, whose heads cock slightly to the side and whose brows furrow as you ask your questions. You are so dang cute. Not to say I don't take you seriously. I do.

Here's why I narrowed it to disappointment.

My reason for focusing on disappointment for core SIDE practice #2 is because of its connection with core SIDE practice #1. Like we saw when we looked at the first core practice, people stop coming to church when they're no longer as fascinated with the church they were initially enamoured with. There's usually disappointment involved when someone pulls herself out of community. There are many reasons for this possible disappointment: the once fascinating pastor makes some jokes that are in bad taste (I've heard this happens in some places); the Sunday school teacher who is doing a great job with your kid is raising a couple of kids of her own who are hard to take; the usher has body odour; the seniors' group is scantily clad; the couple who invited you to church don't sit with you anymore; half of the guys in the men's group are alcoholics, half are addicted to porn, and the other half can't do simple math. The list of what you're disappointed in can get long. You might even get disappointed in a Christian author who missed something on his list of sample disappointments. Whatever the cause is, disappointment is inevitable. We need to be ready with the core SIDE practice of forgiveness so we don't let disappointment pull us out of community.

I want to focus on disappointment not only because it can pull you out of community, but because it can fly under the radar. It's easier to notice when we've been hurt by someone in a major way. The magnitude and the clarity of the offence can make forgiveness easier because you know what the problem is and can deal with it. But when you've been let down in small ways by the Christians around you, you can miss the need to forgive. They haven't *really* hurt you . . . they just disappointed you. You're not angry that their lives don't display the generosity, kindness, and grace, which they should. You aren't mad about the absence of joy, peace, and love—just disappointed.

It seems harmless, but if you've been paying careful attention to the last paragraph, maybe you're sensing something that makes you feel uncomfortable. Re-read it and see if it isn't in danger of starting to sound a little patronizing. Does it sound a little judgy? It does, doesn't it? This is why you need to pay attention to disappointments and forgive them, because if you allow disappointments to pile up, you'll increasingly become a judgmental person.

Judgment is especially dangerous because it's subtle. It disguises as concern for someone, or a desire for personal holiness, or theological purity, or sadness about how others are suffering, when really, it's festering unforgiveness rotting your soul and eroding community. It can fester only because it's disguised, and once it's hidden, it's very hard to deal with because you don't see it for what it is. You think you're being holy, but you're being angry. So you need to get ahead of it by acknowledging the disappointments immediately and forgiving them.

Your regular core SIDE practice is to think of someone who has disappointed you in your church. He did something you didn't think a serious Christian should do. he gossiped, he got drunk, he took the whole summer off of going to small group, he didn't invite you to the party, he was all really friendly when you first came to the church and now seems to avoid you. Whatever it is. Name your disappointment. And now say out loud that you forgive him.

In my life, this saying out loud sounds like this:

"I forgive Cam for not tithing despite making $300k a year."

"I forgive Fiona for not putting her kids in our private school and helping us make budget."

"I forgive Jean for that critical email where he told me that I was a joke and needed to grow up."

It's important to say it out loud so you can feel sheepish about it. My examples here are real, and as I list them for you, I'm realizing both how petty they sound yet how serious they might become if I don't address them.

Petty because to forgive someone for an angry email is an entirely different level of forgiveness than forgiving an abusive uncle, an absent dad, or an unfaithful spouse. The out loud forgiveness examples above seem hardly worth mentioning when compared to real offences. But it's telling how quickly they all came to mind. As soon as I thought, *I should offer some personal examples of where I'm disappointed,* they were there. They were clearly present in my subconscious and were shaping how I was feeling and thinking about Cam, Fiona, and Jean. My disappointment with them had become the lens through which I would see them until I forgave them. However mild the offence might be, the effect it was having on our church community was not mild. I can't relate to the person until I forgive. Until I forgive, I'm only relating to the part of them that has offended me. That makes community impossible.

The two core practices of SIDE will build your sail. Unforgiveness and isolation shrink your sail. Go it solo for a while, or stop being quick to forgive, and you'll wonder where the wind went. But if you go to church, if you serve the church, if you forgive as the Lord forgives you—both big and small offences—then you will always be able to feel the breeze.

DOWN

DOWN Core Belief: Nothing You Do for Jesus Is Ever Useless

Full disclosure: this core belief comes from 1 Corinthians 15:58 (NLT), where Paul writes: "Nothing you do for the Lord is ever useless." All I did was take his phrase and use it. I'm happy to send him a royalty cheque for using his idea, but I'm not sure where to send it. Perhaps the Vatican?

Paul's claim here is remarkable. He's saying that why you do something matters more than what you do. That the road to heaven is paved with the right motivations. His claim is that if your desire is to honour Jesus with what you're doing, if your act of service is done because it's a way to show Jesus you love him, then whatever you do will matter. This is remarkable, because it can often seem like what we try to do not only doesn't matter, but it's a failure. Paul promises otherwise. He promises what you are doing will bear fruit. It will change something. It will help God's UPSIDEDOWN dream come true. It is not useless.

Please note that the promise assures you eventual effectiveness, not merely that you will make God pleased. It's a fine thing to please God. But in this case, there is more promised. It would be wrong to imagine yourself in front of God, standing amidst the shambles of your embarrassed and failed efforts, being assured by him that despite how useless all your work was, he still loves you. No, the promise is that as you stand before him, you will be celebrating success as you see how even those most miserable of failures have been redeemed and powerfully used in service of the UPSIDEDOWN dream, provided your motivation was pure. The promise here is not that he loves you enough to take your elementary art class pictures and hang them on his fridge—it's that he will take those crude drawings and make them masterpieces that encourage and challenge other people.

This is comforting, at least on the surface, but if I know anything about you by now, it's that you are a person who goes below the surface. You pride yourselves on your self-awareness. You constantly examine your subterranean depths, and because of this, you know how terribly hard it is to have pure motivation. How exactly do you know when you're doing something for Jesus, and how do you know when you're performing for less holy reasons? Sigh . . . sometimes I wish you weren't so clever and introspective. It would make this easier. But I'm stuck with you, so let's unpack some of the complexities that come when we ask questions about what's really motivating us.

Let's first consider some of the possible motivations we might have. Do we do it because of the attention we might receive? Are we trying to get a date? Are we trying to get our wife in a pleasant enough mood to approve the purchase of a new mountain bike? When we drive by the window of the family we gave the Christmas hamper to and take a peek inside, what do we feel? For sure, it feels great, but why? Perhaps the warm feelings come as you feel God's approval wash over you because you're acting like your Father in heaven. Or the swell of happiness might be because the humble scene reminds you of your advantageous financial situation, which makes the generosity possible in the first place. Maybe the family you've helped only needed help because the father couldn't keep a job. You've kept your job. You're assistant manager even! Maybe the positive vibes you feel are due to a sense of superiority. You're glad you don't have to depend on others the way these people depend on you. Or it could be that you feel great because your kids are sitting in the back seat and asked why you slowed down to look into the living room of that house. "Oh, I wasn't going to say anything, but . . ." You can feel the respect level for old pops reach an all-time, back-seat high. You could wonder about motivation like this forever, such is your rigorous commitment to self-awareness. I don't want to minimize your introspection. There's a lot going on inside all of us, and it would be naïve to assume we're ever purely motivated by God to do anything.

That doesn't mean we can't spin a few scenarios that might help us purify us our motivation. One of the easiest ways to tell that your motivation is compromised is to ask: "How would I feel if the situation of the person I was helping improved?" Would you be truly glad, or would you struggle with no longer being needed and miss the ego strokes that come with being relied on?

I think of a friend of mine whose husband was a long-time alcoholic who got sober. You'd imagine she would be thrilled. He used to be a burden, but now he was helpful. He would shovel the driveway. He would take out the recycling. He would ensure the bills were paid on time. This new version of him made her furious. She missed the old drunk. Why? Her ego needed him to be sick for her to feel worth something. She helped him not to move him to health, but to make her feel smugly superior. If you find yourself feeling annoyed when people get healthy, you have reason to suspect your motivation.

Another way to know your motivation is off is if you can't keep your good deeds a secret. Be suspicious if you always manage to find a way to sneak in how you are helping people. It can be hard to spot because many of us get very good at dropping hints. We don't necessarily notice what we're doing. Like when the person being baptized didn't mention you in their testimony, and you said to someone later, "I feel really good about the role I got to play here. By God's grace, I managed to help them along in a way that has them relying on God and not me. I mean, they didn't even mention me in their speech. How amazing is that?" Pretty amazing. Almost as impressive as your ability to take credit in a holy sounding way. The best among us will add something like, "And you know, it was also a chance for me to thank God for how he has worked in my life. I used to be the sort of person whose feelings would be hurt by not being mentioned, especially if I had played a significant role in someone's life. I'm grateful I'm not there anymore. I'm able to simply celebrate, even if I don't get any credit." Ouch! It's hard to determine our true motivation, but if you find your need for credit or recognition overpowers your ability to keep your good deeds a secret, it's a sure sign something is off motivation-wise.

That it's hard to know our real motivation, or to ensure 100 per cent pure motives, should not stop you from trying to help others, not for a second. Jesus knows your limitations and still invites you to help him turn the world UPSIDEDOWN. Besides, as you begin to try to do things with the right motivation, you move closer to being able to naturally possess the right motivations. Feeling Jesus's pride in you is a considerable reward all on its own, but it also helps purify your motive. It has a cleansing effect; it burns away the lesser rewards of ego. When you feel his attentiveness, you don't need attention from others. You don't need lesser rewards, because you're receiving what you really long for—the attention of Jesus.

Paul's encouragement not only reminds you to pay attention to your motivation, but it also helps you not grow weary when you don't see the hoped-for results of your work. It keeps us going to know that, even though our efforts might not result in what we thought they should, they weren't in vain. Having this truth available to seize will be a lifesaver when you feel like you're drowning in futility, like when you mustered up the courage to talk with a friend about Jesus. You assumed, because of how compelling you found Jesus yourself, that your conversation would be, if not a significant spiritual milestone for her, at least the beginning of a new spiritual journey. But that was two years ago, and despite your best attempts at witnessing, every time you even come close to bringing Jesus up again, she changes the subject. Or maybe what feels futile is the Friday nights you give up in order to be a small group leader for the Grade 9 boys at church. It has been three months of you hoping the conversation moves beyond farts and video games; nothing of merit has visibly happened. It sure as heck seems like your efforts are in vain.

Or maybe your partner is not at all interested in following Jesus. There's some tension in your relationship because he didn't marry a Christian but is now stuck with one. Of course, your goal is to make it feel like he's not stuck at all. In fact, you want so badly for him to see and appreciate the changes in you. You want him to eventually have to admit that you're a better person for having Jesus in your life. But this isn't even close to happening; instead, every week it's a fight when you want to go to church and he wants to take the kids to the lake.

In these moments of despair, it might seem like a shallow self-talk trick to tell yourself that "Nothing I do for Jesus is in vain!" It's hard to imagine it changing your mood in the moment, and especially hard to see how it would give you the endurance to keep slogging it out as the frustrations pile up. But it does work! Not quite like you might imagine it might, but all God's truths, when you hold on to them stubbornly, always manage to provide what you need in difficult moments. I know this because I'm no stranger to these frustrations. I have been a pastor for twenty years. I get frustrated with a lack of results every single week!

Take the Sunday sermon. Every week I preach a sermon that I hope results in more than it does. I have high hopes for these mornings, and this is good. No one wants a disillusioned preacher mailing it every Sunday. But my high hopes create vulnerability, and the emotional roller coaster takes a predictable dip every Sunday afternoon. Some weeks the disappointment is harder to take than others. I remember one time a young man whose marriage was falling apart hurried to the front to talk to me post-sermon. I was excited. The sermon was about marriage, in part because the man and his wife were on my heart as I had prepared and prayed. He had proven to be a tough nut to crack thus far. Any conversations about his marriage weren't about how to make it better but about what she was doing wrong. When he sprinted to the front to talk to me at the end of a sermon about marriage, one where I had gently tweaked the content in the hopes it would connect with him, I was hopeful. I thought maybe God had finally gotten through.

He sat down next to me and said, "In your sermon . . ."

The baby leapt within me (Lk 1:41)! I was excited! He was listening! I leaned in to hear more and he continued.

"In your sermon, you mentioned a product you had ordered online that did a great job of reconditioning the leather upholstery in your car. But I didn't catch the name."

I went full-on kickboxer. I delivered a sweet roundhouse kick to the side of his head. I'm joking, but I was that frustrated. I was too frustrated to risk doing any more than pretending it was a great joy to tell him the name of the product; you would have thought I received a commission for it. He jotted the name down and headed home to his miserable marriage and hurting family to recondition some leather.

When my anger faded, which it did quickly, I was left with disappointment, and a reason to wonder about my motivation. That's why this story is a fitting one to end this section. Sure, I was also sad about his marriage, but embarrassingly, that wasn't the biggest emotional part of it for me. I know my motivation is off when my pride gets hurt. Pride is as sure an indicator of a motivation problem as any. How many years have I been in this church? How many divorces? How many messed up kids because of how their parents relate to each other? Shouldn't I be able to see more fruit? More success? Emotional fatigue set in as I realized the double whammy of not only having no tangible results in front of me, but also that I appear to still be primarily motivated by achieving success. I really wanted his marriage to get better, but I also really wanted to be the one who helped him do it.

There will be moments when a) you don't want the person you are helping to get better, b) you can't keep a secret, and c) your pride becomes obvious. In those moments, you will know your motivation is off and what you're doing is in danger of being useless, no matter what you might be seeing in front of you. This is where your self-awareness can help you. The moment you realize what's going on, you pray: "Help me, Jesus! I really want to be motivated by my love for you. I confess I am seeking validation, recognition, and ego strokes here, but I just want you. Sorry. Forgive me and reassure me through your Holy Spirit that even today's failures will be redeemed as I allow you to purify to my motivation." It's the kind of prayer our compassionate Lord delights to answer because he doesn't want you to waste a moment of your life. He wants everything you do to matter.

DOWN Core Practice #1: Tithing

I toyed with making the DOWN Core Practice #1 "generosity" instead of "tithing." My reasons for being tempted to move in that direction are obvious. Most Christians don't tithe and don't intend to tithe, so for many of them the challenge to tithe puts them on the defensive. I expect I'll be fighting an uphill battle, but I still chose to talk specifically about money. The main reason for this choice is that I agree with Jesus when he says you can tell where someone's heart is based solely on what they spend their money on. When he says this, he's articulating a rule for reality that I have personally never seen broken. Remember how Jesus never has opinions, he only describes how it is? That's what he's doing here (Lk 12:34). When I think of the people I know who are financially generous, it's not a stretch to consider them people whose hearts are, as we say, "in the right place." I want to focus on money because structured financial generosity will transform your heart like few other activities will. Your heart is at the mercy of your wallet.

Financial generosity starts with you giving a significant portion of your income to the church you attend. And if you're thinking to yourself, *How predictable. Of course a pastor would say that*, please note that I am counselling you to give the money to your church, not mine. I already got your money, because you bought this book. You paid for this Cuban cigar and the champagne-filled hot tub I'm sitting in as I smoke it. I'm joking. For the record, the cigar is Honduran, and the tub is filled with cold Budweiser.

I'm joking to try to lower the tension. But I don't want to distract from the challenge I'm presenting. You need to systematically be financially supporting your church. Now, if you can't in good conscience support your church—like, if the pastor is spending money on $1,500 sneakers, or drugs, has a garage full of European collector cars, or sits smoking cigars in tubs filled with cold Budweiser—then find a church you can support.

Not to say you need to find a perfect church. You won't always agree with everything done in the church, but you should make sure you find one with strong financial accountability structures and where the pastor's lifestyle isn't that much higher or lower than the average person in the congregation. Once you find that church, you should tithe, even on those Sundays when the worship band is off key.

Let's dive into the resistance I imagine you're feeling. I suspect by now you have googled "tithing" and found it to refer to 10 per cent of your income and you're thinking, *No wonder Uncle Nathan didn't want to explain what it meant.* Does this really deserve to be one of the core practices? Yes. Again, I'm looking at what practices are the ones that cause the other ones to fall in line. I am concerned with which ones have the most ripple effects.

One of the ripple effects of tithing is how it bonds you to community. Consider how your level of belonging is always connected to your level of sacrifice. Ever been on a team where one player just sort of coasts along? The rest of the team is sitting in the locker room post-game, dripping in sweat and lamenting the loss or celebrating the win. Win or lose, the sense of camaraderie and community is connected to the effort they put in to achieve the same goal. The poor schlub who didn't break a sweat isn't going to feel what the rest of the team feels. In fact, the person who hasn't done what the others did will feel sheepish and guilty and sense a distance between himself and the other players. He'll feel like he never really belonged on the team. And the truth is, he didn't, because people on that particular team all committed in a way that the one individual didn't.

I believe strongly enough in this to check the generosity levels of our staff and board at our church. Most of the time this is a routine checkup that requires no follow-up on my part. But in the rare times when we find someone who isn't generous, her identity is no surprise. She is exactly who I would have guessed was not tithing. She was disconnected from the team and lacking in passion for mission. No kidding! Every other staff person and board member was giving sacrificially and generously, and the person sitting next to them wasn't. What do you expect to feel when you're that person? No wonder there were problems. When someone who is all in tries to do life at a deep level with someone who is only kinda in, it doesn't work. Like the team example, it isn't a matter of not belonging.

It's a matter of not committing at the same level as your community. You would quickly feel you belonged if you put some skin in the game. Tithing helps you belong.

I hope it's clear by now that by "belong" I don't mean you belong because you're paying the same membership dues as everyone else. No, the tithing shifts your heart toward, and opens it to, the people around you. There's now a compatibility between you and the people around you that wasn't there before. The ripple effects of tithing are one of the reasons I'm challenging you with it; I want the church to be the family for you that it can be. I want you to belong.

The other reason I want you to tithe is because it's a wise investment. It's an investment God guarantees. Remember, nothing you do for God is done in vain. Other investments are often in vain. Your retirement savings are vulnerable to the fluctuations in the market. They're certainly not guaranteed. The most guaranteed investment is to invest in the UPSIDEDOWN dream. In one of his more pointed jokes, Jesus directs us to not invest our money in what is temporary. That isn't the joke. The joke is in the image he uses to illustrate what we're doing when we do. He wonders why someone would be so committed to purchasing what either moths or rust will chew away (Mt. 6:19–20). He makes us giggle at the stupidity of choosing to lease a new truck, or refinance to reno the kitchen, when it compromises our ability to tithe. The images he chooses make it obvious what we ought to do. Why buy what a bug is going to eat when it keeps you from spending money on something that will be around for millions of years and give you increasing levels of joy and pride? Ha, ha ... moths. Like we would ever do that, Jesus. You so funny.

DOWN Core Practice #2: Lift the Burdens of the Oppressed in Your Neighbourhood

The second core practice for DOWN is to help people who need help. Life can be tremendously hard for people. I'm not talking here about how the renovation is taking way longer and is over budget, or your power-hungry boss, or the frustration you have when the fridge breaks the week after the warranty expires. Yes, these are annoyances that test our character to some extent, but as our character grows as we fire on all syllables, these little interruptions in the flow of our day don't really affect our mood.

I'm not talking about what are sometimes referred to as "First World problems." No, the burdens I'm talking about are the issues that are more significant than fridge warranties expiring. While burdens like caring for aging parents or driving someone to cancer treatments are significant ways to help people, and Christians do need to help bear these sorts of burdens, they're not what I have in mind.

On my mind are the people who are struggling because of systemic racial oppression and the cyclical patterns of family trauma, abuse, and poverty that flow from that original oppression. You're not firing on the DOWN syllable until there's a place in your life you can point to that shows you are legitimately trying to help people working to break free from these chains.

These are difficult waters to navigate, because even when our hearts are in the right place, we might not know what the path ahead looks like. We can feel paralyzed because we're all aware that helping can hurt, lives are complex, we are not expert counsellors, poverty gurus, or dextrous enough to cross the social, economic, and racial lines that are often involved. Yes, the issues are complex and require diligent thinking. Lifting these kinds of burdens requires wisdom.

A common definition for wisdom is to see it as "the appropriate and practical application of knowledge." That is not a bad definition, but I prefer to define wisdom as this: wisdom is what happens when love and courage embrace. Lifting the kind of burdens I'm talking about requires love and courage. The love that compels us to not turn away. The courage to move toward the hurt. The love that purifies our motives. The courage to take personal responsibility and not always delegate to others more suited to tackle these issues than us. It's important to notice how subtle these delegating workarounds can be.

A couple of years ago, my church set a record in Canada—at least as far as I know. In one Sunday, our church of several hundred families sponsored nearly two hundred Compassion Canada children in the Philippines. For context, our attendance that day (including children) was about five hundred people, so it reflects maybe two hundred families in attendance. What I'm saying is basically every single family and person at our church responded.

I was blessed but not surprised. We are a church that understands the importance of firing on all syllables; in fact, the UPSIDEDOWN idea forms our weekly rhythms. One week is UP, the next is SIDE, and then DOWN. That we can hit the DOWN syllable was obvious on that record-setting Sunday. And truly, the dominant emotion I had was pride. I absolutely loved how our church family proved itself to be the kind of group that responds to people who need help. But as excited as I was about our response, I couldn't deny there was a hollow longing about the whole thing for me, which remains to this day.

The longing comes from the fact that our town is surrounded by Indigenous communities, two large Ojibway reservations and two smaller Dakota ones. Even discounting the demographic of the surrounding area, which would include these reserves, our town population alone is nearly one-third Indigenous. It's wrong to merely say our Indigenous neighbours bear the scars of several centuries of white oppression—wrong because very little has scarred over. The wounds are still open.

In the centre of these communities sits our church. A church that leaps at the chance to help those who need it every time it comes on our radar. A church that is ensuring that two hundred Filipino families on the other side of the world have clean water, medical attention, proper nourishment, and access to secondary and post-secondary education. This caring church with a heart of gold has about six Indigenous people who are a part of our community with any regularity, and a couple of those have white spouses or partners and so, in a sense, have "married in." It is frustrating. It is puzzling.

It would be less frustrating in some ways if I felt like most of our church members were closet racists who are happy to throw money at problems on the other side of the planet because then they can keep their white hands clean. There might be a few like that. The church is a hospital for sinners and not a museum for saints, so I wouldn't be surprised to find some racist embers still smouldering in our midst. But if they stick around as part of our church for long enough, those embers will be stamped out under Jesus's boot. The God of peace has promised to crush Satan under our feet, and racism is satanic. Our church wants to crush it.

So it isn't that we lack care or desire. I don't think. But the fact remains that the most specific burdens we are geographically situated to help with are exactly the ones we can't seem to lift. I've thought about this a great deal and I wonder if we are maybe lacking courage. A lack of courage might explain why we find it difficult to build relational bridges with Indigenous people in our city but respond with generosity to an institution like Compassion Canada. It takes little courage to help people you don't know or won't ever see. But God's intention is for you to bring the UPSIDEDOWN dream to exactly where you already are. This is why this DOWN core practice emphasizes "in your neighbourhood."

Please don't misunderstand me. Of course it's good to give money to worthy causes to further their mandate and alleviate global suffering. Please don't stop that, but please do see the potential is there for you to feel you are "making a difference" when all along you're not making the difference God wants you to make. God wants you to be a redemptive force in your neighbourhood. He wants you to address the burdens right under your nose, because no one else notices them. You are in the geographical location you are in, in the town you are in, in the job you are in, to make the UPSIDEDOWN dream come true right in front of you.

When I talk like this, people ask me where to start. It's the right question in some ways. Certainly a better one than "What does this look like down the road?" or "Will this be sustainable for me?" The focus on what might come is paralyzing because it has you overthinking and strategizing. You don't have to overthink. Start with friendship. Focusing on friendship reduces the risk of making people projects we manipulate toward our eventual goal. It's probably healthier to not have a goal in mind. You can't manipulate someone toward an endgame you haven't articulated. When you don't know what you're doing, it's hard to have people feel like they are projects. When you don't know what you're doing is when you get to know people's names and stories, and you find yourself asking them what you should be doing, because you don't really know what else to do. The "Where do I start?" question is helpful, provided you don't use it as an excuse to wait for the perfect place to begin.

Seek to befriend someone who is carrying a burden in your neighbourhood. And if you don't see anyone, look a little harder, I can't imagine you live in the one place in the world where there is no violence, racism, or poverty. It will take some intentional effort to move in the direction I'm calling you to move, but it won't take much effort to see the direction you are called to move if you allow yourself to see it. Take your cues from your tears. When your eyes start to water up, you know you are looking in the right direction.

I work with a guy who cries at the drop of a hat. He will announce an upcoming potluck and weep like a father welcoming home a prodigal son. So maybe for him tears are not the best sign. But for me, when my usually dry eyes well up with tears of passion or frustration, I know I'm being called by God to move.

It happened eight years ago. It was the first day of school, and since our church also is the home of Westpark School, there was some serious excitement in the building as a couple hundred kids were buzzing around. At lunch time, I wandered through the lobby by the reception desk and saw half a dozen Indigenous students in Grade 9 standing by the doors. They were scanning the parking lot as if waiting to be picked up. I was curious. Most of these kids were from a small reserve twenty minutes out of town where they attended school with friends and family until they graduated from Grade 8. I was surprised they would have friends or relatives in town who would be picking them up for lunch the first day of school. I went over to chat with them.

Before I continue with my story, I should take the opportunity here to say that our school is an example to our church. The last few years, our Westpark School student body has been approximately one-third Indigenous. We've been privileged to host powwow dancers and drum groups at our chapels. Westpark School is a place where God's UPSIDEDOWN dreams for planet Earth are coming true. When you walk the halls, you notice a lightness and joy. This is because every classroom and office contains a staff person who is a burden lifter. I believe what God is beginning to do at Westpark School will eventually change all of Canada.

Back to my story about tears. The first day at a new school is hard, even when you aren't an Indigenous kid from a small reservation trying to get a handle on the social dynamics and schedule of this white-person-run church school. I tried to make conversation, but it was difficult to get much of a response from them. During the time spent trying to chat, it became clear they weren't waiting for anyone. Rather, they were giving the impression that they had something on the go, that they were people who had people coming to find them, and not scared kids feeling isolated and terrified.

When that sunk in, I started to cry. Like really cry. Embarrassing head-to-the-bathroom-late-for-my-next-meeting kind of cry. The Holy Spirit nailed me and I was totally blindsided by emotion. And then when I did go to my next meeting and explained why I was late, I started bawling again. It was the heart of God welling up in me, and his heart is so much bigger than my heart that there needed to be some release. The release of the pressure came out my tear ducts.

My love prompted me to do something. The next day I started a weekly lunch with the Indigenous kids in our high school. Most don't stay for more than a year. Some transfer to another school. Some are expelled for bad behaviour. Some stop coming. Some get pregnant. Some keep coming, and I get to eat lunch once a week with them for four years. Some go to university. Some ask me to help them get a job. One has ended up living in my house with his little brother for the last year and a half because they had nowhere else to go.

Once a month or so, I run into one of these kids who are no longer at our school. There have been about fifty of them whom I've gotten to have lunch with over the years, and our town is small, so paths cross frequently. Recently I ran into Nathan (he has the same name as me) at the beer store (I am there witnessing), and he showed me a picture of his kid and updated me on how he was doing. Always when I see these kids they are trying to "do better" and to "make good choices," but the deck remains stacked against them. And always when I see them I blink back tears, as I do writing this, and feel about as close to God as I ever do, because my sail is growing.

My staff gets a kick out of how emotional I get when it comes to this. Most of the time they experience me much like I suppose you have experienced me in this book: cerebral, logical, chasing weird rabbit trails, sarcastic, abrupt shifts in tone, and delighting in the absurd. But then I start talking about Indigenous kids and I turn into a ball of mush. I can go to a funeral and sit stoic through the whole thing. But after five minutes of playing catch with an Indigenous teenager, I risk getting hit in the head with the ball because my eyes are all blurred with tears.

Now, this is not to brag. Oh, my goodness, no. If anything, it's more of a confession that for the first thirty-some years of my life, I had such a heavy accent on the UP and SIDE syllables that I didn't feel much wind. Despite my decades-long sponsorship of children, and faithful tithing, my sail was miserably small, and I had no idea why. I was that person searching and longing for a powerful experience of the Holy Spirit. So I prayed more. I learned more. I asked for more. I loyally attended small group and weekly accountability groups. There was not much stirring of wind. Then I learned the names and stories of a few Indigenous kids and found myself in the middle of a Holy Spirit hurricane. My DOWN side of the sail was very small, basically represented only by faithfully tithing.

This gust of wind shouldn't have surprised me. Around that time, I discovered Isaiah 58. It is an UPSIDEDOWN passage. It showed me what was wrong with my life and showed me the path I would have to walk to fix my life. The writer of Isaiah 58 is addressing a group of people who are confused about the lack of power in their lives to bring about change. They lack the presence of God, they lack momentum, and they don't know why. The problem, says the author, is they are accenting the wrong syllables.

The author almost taunts them, but it's not really a taunting because he immediately gives them hope. You sing your songs. You bring your money. But you don't give a rat's ass about the people who need help. Not really. But if you were to start . . . oh good God, what you would experience! The momentum, the intimacy, and the joy. The rewards. You would become someone who could rebuild the ruined lives. God would empower you to restore families.

If you don't know where to start, pay attention to when the tears flow. If the tears aren't flowing, ask God for a soft heart and open eyes. God wants you passionate about his UPSIDEDOWN dream and will break your heart if you ask him to. He want you to lift the burdens of the oppressed in your neighbourhood.

Excursus: Anna

They call it the "cry of dereliction." It's when Jesus shouts out "My God, my God, why have you forsaken me?"

We had just spent twenty minutes coaxing conversation out of three high-school students who attend our weekly lunch. Tamara is a godsend in these lunches, as her ability to pepper people with questions is matched by her absolute unwillingness to give up when 90 per cent of her questions are met with silence or grunts.

No one from the reserve has graduated since 1989. We know eating soup and buns once a week won't change that. I'm not sure why we do it, but I know after every lunch hour I am misty-eyed and I feel close to Jesus. So I imagine and trust something is happening that I can't see. Nothing you do is ever in vain, right?

Shaun is a regular. He dresses all in black and looks like he showers once a week. It took a full year before Shaun would look me in the eye and another five months before he would say, "Hi, Nathan." On rare occasions our conversation stumbles onto something. Shaun has no dad. I know his mom died five years ago. I went to the funeral. He and his three younger siblings are being raised by his older sister. Big sis did a heroic job with four younger siblings until she ended up with a drug-dealer boyfriend and a baby.

We were talking about how sometimes the way people dress can reveal how they feel about themselves.

"What do you think, Shaun?"

"Chhh! You think I LIKE dressing in long sleeve black sweaters all summer? I'm ashamed."

My God . . . this is his first full sentence.

Anna is more talkative than Shaun but wasn't in class this morning. Although now she is here at lunch but not eating. We offered her a sandwich but she wasn't hungry. She just wanted to talk. That's nice. Tamara started asking them all what kind of person they would want to marry. The answers are slow and predictable. Nice people. People who aren't cruel. Anna figures sarcasm is OK—just not too much. We should stay away from people who punch us. We should probably not drink or do drugs, because we can end up with others who do.

The same conversations we've had in the last three years with Shauna who ended up at fifteen moving in with a twenty-one-year-old guy. The same conversations we had with Mitch, who dropped out of Grade 10 and parties every night. The same conversations we had with Margaret, who had a black eye the last time I saw her. My God, my God...

The clock turns to 1:10 p.m. and lunch is over. You can see out in the main lunchroom all the other high-school students, who have better things to do than eat sandwiches with old people, going back to class.

Off goes Shaun, but here sits Anna.

"My mom brought me in for the afternoon because she wants me to talk to you."

I'm gonna hear she's pregnant. And John is the father. John who is seventeen and reads like he's seven. John who has a short fuse. So I'm braced.

"My cousin died last night."

(Whew... guilty relief.)

"He hung himself."

(...oh...)

And then a sound.

It starts as laughter in the pits of hell, but by the time it has worked its way through a young woman's lungs, diaphragm, throat, and tongue, it has no merriment left at all. Just audible pain. Cold, smacking agony. And when enough composure comes for her to form words, she says, "I think he did it because they took his baby away. They thought he was hitting him. But the baby just has a tumour."

Apparently a restraining order was in place; the girlfriend felt threatened. Baby Marcus is in the hospital being treated for something. We don't know if it's a tumour or injuries. We do know Anna's cousin, the father, is dead. His name is Brad. He hung for two days before they noticed him. My God, my God, why...

When he was little, Anna's family used to have Brad live with them. When Brad was three, he would snuggle up in the big bed with Anna's dad and big brother Marvin. I don't hear any of these memories. All I can hear is the sound she made. I've heard it in the pages of scripture, I've just never heard it:

"My God, my God, why have you forsaken?"

I pastor because, as impossible as it all is sometimes, I don't believe he has. But God, I wish we only had to wait three days for this to get fixed. She made the sound I feel most days if I pay attention. Father, have mercy on us sinners NOW.

Nothing you do for the Lord is ever in vain is a kind of mercy.

PARTY/CONCLUSION/EPILOGUE

(Happiness Is a By-product)

Our church takes the UPSIDEDOWN idea and weaves it into our community life. Each week is dedicated to a different syllable. On UP weeks, our Sunday service includes special UP components, and our midweek small groups do as well. Our staff stays on syllable in our various meetings, and the youth group does the same. Each week has a slightly different flavour depending on the syllable we're on. We march along week to week UP-SIDE-DOWN.

But people who attend our church know there is one more week I haven't covered in the book yet. They will tan my hide if I don't get to it. That's what happens to us humble country parsons when our congregations get mad. Doesn't matter how many babies we've safely delivered—we are always one mistake away from a good old prairie hide tanning.

They are correct. There is one more syllable I haven't shared with you. But here in the twilight of our journey together (trying to be poetic about the book ending—neither of us are dying), I will. The reason I haven't gotten to this last thing is because it doesn't quite flow out of the big anastatoo idea the way UPSIDEDOWN does. It's more like the result of the UPSIDEDOWN life than an ingredient. More like a by-product than something you do, so it doesn't quite fit. Plus, it isn't one syllable. It is two, and that kind of messes things up for me. Might seem odd to you that I get hung up on how things fit or don't, since I haven't exactly established myself in this book as strict linear thinker. But no, underneath the playful chaos of these chapters is a relatively firm loom on which I have woven this exquisite tapestry. And it was hard to find room on the loom for this last thread.

But here we are in the conclusion of the book, and I might as well throw my outline to the wind and tell you about this last "syllable," because you're going to discover it anyway. The UPSIDEDOWN life will naturally take you there. The missing syllable? PARTY! If you have any issues with it, take it up with our associate pastor, the weepy, potluck-loving, Tubbz Kehler. It was his idea.

I don't think you should have any problem with it. It's a great idea to tag PARTY onto UPSIDEDOWN, but maybe we should have kept the one syllable thing going and gone with JOY.

The idea of tagging PARTY on the end of UPSIDEDOWN is that the natural result of having an UP SIDE DOWN cadence in your life will be that your life begins to take on the celebratory tone of a party. Firing on all syllables leads to a lightness of being that allows you to truly celebrate and enjoy your life. I say "truly" because we have all been at parties that consist of people yelling at each other over the music, "Isn't this FUN?" and responding with "SO FUN!" over and over. This is not "truly." This is not an authentic experience. This is not celebratory. This is desperate and forced. When something is truly fun, we rarely have to remind each other how much fun we're having every few minutes. No, when we're truly enjoying something, there is a depth of experience we don't want to interrupt by trying to explain it to ourselves or validate it to others. It doesn't occur to us to interrupt it. There is no need. If we do have to interrupt the natural flow of joy to remark on it, those interruptions are indications that we have not yet found what we're looking for. The PARTY I'm talking about is not a moment you chase and then attempt to validate with a selfie. No, you don't chase this party. It comes to you as a reward. Joy is the reward for living the UPSIDEDOWN life, and joy is waiting for you.

So go build your sail. Adopt the three core beliefs and dive into the six core practices. You have everything you need to build a massive sail. You really do. Get going and let joy find you. I know it will. Because it found me.

My friend Josh was sitting with me on my deck about four years ago. We were puffing on cigars. This is not something we condone but rather a necessary thing to do to keep the Manitoba mosquitos away. He was sharing with me a dream he had about starting a flight school for at-risk kids. Since he was a career military pilot and flight instructor, this was not an entirely ridiculous dream. Not like my dream to win the world sumo wrestling championships in the over-forty lightweight division. I shouldn't make light of it. His dream was born out of careful prayer and attentiveness to God's voice. He and his wife, Ashleigh, began to pray about it consistently for the next three years. It was an UP dream.

As they shared their dream with an increasingly large circle of praying and supportive friends, it became a SIDE dream. Josh and Ashleigh's commitment to the SIDE syllable kept them embedded in a community which refined, and propelled them toward, their dream.

Then, courageously, this young couple with two little children went to the bank and secured the money to finance it. They put so much skin in the game. You didn't have to wonder where their hearts were . . . their money told you. This was not the only way it was a DOWN dream. It also focused exclusively on teaching at-risk Indigenous kids to fly. This last summer, Eagle's Wings Flight School had its first cohort of students, and Josh got to teach six teens how to fly.

It gets better. Since the students came from Indigenous backgrounds, and Josh created space for cultural education and celebration, his volunteer pilots and lecturers got a new appreciation of the richness of Indigenous culture. The project represented partnerships between local child welfare agencies, private schools, churches, the local military base, and Dakota and Ojibway elders and teachers. It was as UPSIDEDOWN an event as I have ever seen. Anastatoo all over the place. Josh could have been arrested because of the way he was knocking down established barriers.

One of the students in his program is Clicky, my foster son. Wisdom and propriety prevent me from detailing the sorts of things my boy has had to go through in his life, but they have been weighty and many. A scholarship form he was filling out for university required him to share a time where he faced hardship and what his response was. He asked me, "Which time would actually be appropriate to share?" He carries burdens. He is someone in my neighbourhood whose burden I have lifted, and on Saturday morning at 8 a.m., he was going to fly for the first time.

Tamara and I went out to the wire fence beside the runway. We found Ashleigh there. Ashleigh is the most attentive listener I've ever met. Her eyes are wide, and she focuses them on you, and you feel heard. This morning her eyes were as wide as ever but brimming with joy; ours were too.

Clicky taxied along and I thought about the way God shaped me over the years as I worked to live a life firing on all syllables.

I thought about UP as the prayers and the Bible reading helped reshape my perspective. To help me resist the easy pull of safety and low risk. The quick and clear answer to prayer when I asked Jesus if we should open our home to two foster sons.

I thought about SIDE. The small group I was in with Josh. The two guys I meet with every week who don't let me have any secrets or get away with something stupid. I thought of our church and how the people in it have been faithful to attend and faithful to forgive. The strong health of a church that allows for Josh and Ashleigh to have courage. The community that has been so patient with me for the last nearly twenty years as I slowly grow and mature to become more and more like Jesus.

I thought about DOWN. I thought about the generosity of all the volunteers in the Eagle's Wings program, taking their holidays to serve. I thought about Josh's bank account and how much more strain there is on it now than there was a year ago. I thought about the Indigenous kids learning to fly who bear the scars of the way their ancestors were treated. The alcoholism. The abuse. The racism. I thought about Anna and all the other kids I have tried to help but whose names I've forgotten because when they fall off the radar, they fall way off. I thought about all the times I've wandered out across the river of racial divide and almost drowned because I didn't know what to say, didn't know how to help the right way, didn't know when to shut up, but kept trying to swim because love compels you to go where it compels you to go.

Then the little plane turned ninety degrees and started slowly building speed down the runway. Until a young man had enough momentum behind him to take flight. I felt something I never had before. I was about to burst. I think it was because my sail had never been bigger. The wind was blowing, and I swear to God it felt like every single bit of it was hitting me.

I turned to Tamara and said, "I've chased this feeling my whole life."

I've had more of those moments in the last ten years as my sail gets bigger and bigger. This is what it means to grow and follow. This is what is waiting for you in increasing measure.

Joy is a by-product of the UPSIDEDOWN life.

Go get it.

You know what to do.

Printed in Canada